W9-DDX-367

3 4028 05780 5609

HARRIS COUNTY PUBLIC LIBRARY

363.349 Har
Harper, Kristine
Hurricane Andrew

$35.00
ocm55665272

ENVIRONMENTAL DISASTERS

Hurricane Andrew

Kristine Harper, Ph.D.

☑®
Facts On File, Inc.

Hurricane Andrew

Copyright © 2005 by Facts On File, Inc.

All rights reserved. No part of this book may be reproduced or utilized in any form or by any means, electronic or mechanical, including photocopying, recording, or by any information storage or retrieval systems, without permission in writing from the publisher. For information, contact:

Facts On File, Inc.
132 West 31st Street
New York NY 10001

Library of Congress Cataloging-in-Publication Data

Harper, Kristine
  Hurricane Andrew / Kristine Harper.
    p. cm. — (Environmental disasters)
  Includes bibliographical references and index.
  ISBN 0-8160-5759-1 (hc: acid-free paper)
   1. Hurricane Andrew, 1992. 2. Hurricanes—Florida. 3. Hurricanes—Social aspects—Florida. I. Title. II. Environmental disasters (Facts On File)
QC945.H335 2005
363.34'922—dc22   2004053212

Facts On File books are available at special discounts when purchased in bulk quantities for businesses, associations, institutions, or sales promotions. Please call our Special Sales Department in New York at (212) 967-8800 or (800) 322-8755.

You can find Facts On File on the World Wide Web at
http://www.factsonfile.com

A Creative Media Applications, Inc. Production
Writer: Kristine Harper, Ph.D.
Design and Production: Alan Barnett, Inc.
Editor: Matt Levine
Copy Editor: Laurie Lieb
Proofreader: Tania Bissell
Indexer: Nara Wood
Associated Press Photo Researcher: Yvette Reyes
Consultant: Thomas A. Birkland, Nelson A. Rockefeller College of Public Affairs
    and Policy, University at Albany, State University of New York

Printed in the United States of America

VB PKG   10 9 8 7 6 5 4 3 2 1

This book is printed on acid-free paper.

Contents

Preface

This book is about Hurricane Andrew. From August 22 to August 26, 1992, the hurricane passed over the Bahamas, Florida, and Louisiana. The massive storm left 65 people dead and more than $26 billion worth of damage. The map on the next page shows the route that Andrew took as it traveled on its path of destruction.

Almost everyone is curious about such catastrophic events. An interest in these disasters, as shown by the decision to read this book, is the first step on a fascinating path toward learning how disasters occur, why they are feared, and what can be done to prevent them from hurting people, as well as their homes and businesses.

The word *disaster* comes from the Latin for "bad star." Thousands of years ago, people believed that certain alignments of the stars influenced events on Earth, including natural disasters. Today, natural disasters are sometimes called "acts of God" because no human made them happen. Scientists now know that earthquakes, hurricanes, and volcanic eruptions occur because of natural processes that the scientists can explain much better than they could even a few years ago.

An event is usually called a disaster only if it hurts people. For example, an earthquake occurred along Alaska's Denali fault in 2002. Although this earthquake had a magnitude of 7.9, it killed no one and did little serious damage. But a "smaller" earthquake—with a magnitude below 7.0—in Kobe, Japan, in 1995 did billions of dollars in damage and killed about 5,100 people. This quake was considered a disaster.

A disaster may also damage animals and the environment. The *Exxon Valdez* oil spill in Alaska is considered a disaster because it injured and killed hundreds of birds, otters, deer, and other animals. The spill also killed thousands of fish—which

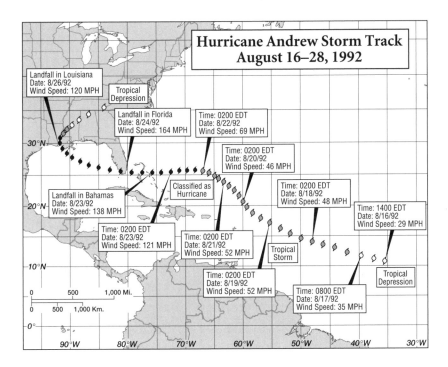

**Hurricane Andrew Storm Track
August 16–28, 1992**

Landfall in Louisiana
Date: 8/26/92
Wind Speed: 120 MPH

Tropical Depression

Landfall in Florida
Date: 8/24/92
Wind Speed: 164 MPH

Time: 0200 EDT
Date: 8/22/92
Wind Speed: 69 MPH

Time: 0200 EDT
Date: 8/20/92
Wind Speed: 46 MPH

30°N

Classified as Hurricane

Time: 0200 EDT
Date: 8/18/92
Wind Speed: 48 MPH

Time: 1400 EDT
Date: 8/16/92
Wind Speed: 29 MPH

Landfall in Bahamas
Date: 8/23/92
Wind Speed: 138 MPH

20°N

Time: 0200 EDT
Date: 8/23/92
Wind Speed: 121 MPH

Time: 0200 EDT
Date: 8/21/92
Wind Speed: 52 MPH

Tropical Storm

10°N

Time: 0200 EDT
Date: 8/19/92
Wind Speed: 52 MPH

Time: 0800 EDT
Date: 8/17/92
Wind Speed: 35 MPH

Tropical Depression

0   500   1,000 Mi.

0   500   1,000 Km.

0°

90°W   80°W   70°W   60°W   50°W   40°W   30°W

many Alaskan fishers rely on to earn their livelihoods—and polluted the places where the fish spawn.

Disasters are also more likely to happen when people make decisions that leave them *vulnerable* to catastrophe. For example, a beachside community is more vulnerable to a hurricane than a community that is inland from the ocean. When people choose where to live, they are also choosing what sort of natural disasters they may experience in the future; they are choosing the sort of risks they are willing to take. People who live on beaches in Florida know that hurricanes may damage or destroy their houses; people who live in certain areas of California know that earthquakes may strike at any time.

The things that people do to make themselves safer from less dangerous natural events, like heavy rains, sometimes actually make the people more vulnerable to bigger disasters. For example, when a dam is built on a river to protect people downstream from floods, the dam may prevent small floods that would otherwise happen once every 25 years. But when a really big storm occurs—the kind that comes once every 100 years—the dam may not be able to hold back the water. Then a surge of water that is even bigger than it would have been without the dam will come rushing down the river and completely destroy all the buildings in the area.

At first, it may seem easy to blame human disasters, like the *Exxon Valdez* spill, on one or a few people. Some observers blame the spill on the captain, who was responsible for the ship. But perhaps the spill was another crewmember's fault. Maybe the blame should fall on Exxon, because that corporation owned the ship. Or maybe all Americans are to blame, because the United States uses a lot of oil for heating houses and driving cars. Finding the "right people" to blame can be difficult. Is it anyone's fault that people suffer from natural disasters? Natural disasters at first appear to be merely unfortunate "acts of God."

This book and the other books in this series will demonstrate that mistakes people made before a disaster often made the disaster worse than it should have been. But they will also show how many people work to lessen the damage caused by disasters. Firefighters, sailors, and police officers, for example, work very hard right after disasters to rescue people, limit additional damage, and help people get back to their normal lives. Behind the scenes are engineers, architects, legislators, scientists, and other citizens working to design new buildings, make new rules about how and where to build buildings, and enforce those rules so that fewer people will have to risk their lives due to disasters.

The books in this series will show what can be done to reduce the chances that people and communities will suffer from natural and human disasters. Everyone has a role to play in making communities safer. The books in this series can show readers how to become part of a growing movement of citizens and experts that can help everyone make good decisions about disasters.

Please note: All metric conversions in this book are approximate.

Introduction

Environmental disasters may be caused by nature or by humans. Some environmental disasters, occurring in densely populated areas, may lead to the loss of human lives and property. Others may occur in more remote areas and lead to the deaths of hundreds of species of plants and animals. One of nature's most violent weather events—the *hurricane*—can spin around harmlessly at sea. However, if it comes ashore, it brings massive destruction to hundreds of square miles of land and all the people, animals, and plants living there. Hurricane Andrew, the most costly hurricane ever to strike the United States, was an environmental disaster.

Until the launching of weather satellites in the early 1960s and the development of fast, accurate, computer-generated hurricane-tracking programs in the late 20th century, it was very difficult to predict the strength and target of hurricanes. Therefore, before the mid-20th century, entire seaside communities might be wiped out by high winds, high waves, and flooding due to heavy rains brought about by a hurricane. The sunny skies and calm seas of a summer day would suddenly become dark and threatening as the hurricane swept over the coastline, bringing death and destruction.

Today, meteorologists can accurately predict where and when a hurricane will strike. They know how strong the winds are and how high the seas will become. Meteorologists even have good estimates of how much rain will fall and can issue flood warnings in advance. Scientific advances allow emergency agencies to order evacuations of coastal areas that will be in danger from the strongest winds and highest seas.

However, in the past 50 years, the number of people living on the coastlines of the United States has grown tremendously. Much more time is needed to evacuate hundreds of thousands of people from large cities than to evacuate a few thousand people from

The increased development of homes and businesses along the nation's coastlines put the population at greater risk from hurricanes and tropical storms. This picture of Miami Beach illustrates just how close thousands of people are to the elements that can become dangerous and deadly in a hurricane. (Photo courtesy of Dave G. Houser/ CORBIS)

small towns. The beauty of sandy beaches on the ocean has encouraged people to build large, expensive homes near the water. These people, and everyone else who builds near the coast in the hurricane areas of the Atlantic Ocean and the Gulf of Mexico, are in danger when these tremendous storms come ashore.

To keep people safe, and to clean up the debris left behind after a hurricane has uprooted trees, blown loose objects through windows, toppled power lines, and contaminated fresh drinking water with dirty floodwater, local, state, and federal government agencies must swing into action immediately. They are aided by private relief organizations, such as the Red Cross and the Salvation Army, which provide emergency shelters and distribute food, fresh water, and enough money to enable people to replace clothing and other necessary items. As more people crowd into coastal areas, the task of providing these services becomes more difficult.

The effect of hurricanes on the natural environment must also be taken into account. Although not a disaster in the human sense, nature is temporarily changed by the high winds and seas. Saltwater may surge inland and poison the land. Large stands of trees may be torn up. Animals that survive the storm may find that their natural habitat no longer exists. Over a number of years, the plants and animals that will resettle these areas may belong to different species than in the past. How much the ecology of the area is changed depends upon the strength of the hurricane, its size, and how long it takes to pass through the area.

Hurricane Andrew explains how and why hurricanes develop around the world. The book then continues by telling the story of one of the strongest hurricanes ever to hit the United States and its immediate and long-term effects on both people and nature. The book concludes with a time line, a chronology of hurricanes, a glossary, and a list of sources (books, articles, and web sites) for further information.

Please note: Glossary words are in italics the first time that they appear in the text. Other words defined in the text may also be in italics.

CHAPTER 1

The Nature of Hurricanes

Hurricanes—when they come ashore, causing death and destruction—are natural disasters. They occur in areas where atmospheric conditions are favorable to their development. Any city or town within an area at risk for hurricanes has a chance of being destroyed each year during hurricane season. Every year, the *Atlantic Ocean hurricane season* opens on June 1 and closes on the last day of November. Anytime during this period, residents of the tropical islands between the United States and South America and people living along the U.S. gulf and Atlantic coasts face the possibility of being hit by a hurricane, or its smaller, less powerful form, the *tropical storm*.

Hurricanes carry massive amounts of water in their thick bands of clouds that can drop over 1 foot (0.3 m) of rain as they pass overhead. Those same *convective clouds* (clouds created by rising, moist air that can grow tens of thousands of feet tall) sometimes produce devastating tornadoes. The combination of high winds and low atmospheric pressure pushes the *storm surge*—large walls of ocean water 30 feet (9.2 m) or more in height—over low-lying islands and coastal areas. Anyone in a hurricane's path is in danger from high floodwaters and the fast-moving winds that uproot trees, break glass, and blow hazardous debris around.

Hurricane Formation and Structure

If weather were a concert, the hurricane would be the star. A hurricane covers more area, is more powerful, and causes more damage over a larger area than any other single weather system. What is a hurricane?

A storm must go through several stages before it is categorized a hurricane. This satellite photograph of a cyclone was taken off the coast of Brazil in March 2004. This storm became the subject of controversy when meteorologists argued over whether it was the first hurricane ever recorded in the South Atlantic. (Photo courtesy of Associated Press)

A hurricane is a low-pressure weather system that is "born" in the *tropics,* generally between 5 and 15 degrees of latitude. (In a *low-pressure system,* the air is rising and circulating in a counter-clockwise direction in the Northern Hemisphere.) The warm ocean water of the tropical summer provides the energy that allows the hurricane to grow from a collection of individual thunderstorms into an organized, spinning mass of clouds.

In order for the hurricane to develop, the ocean's surface temperature must be at least 78°F (25.5°C) down to a depth of 197 feet (60 m). The warm water, combined with the hot air above it, causes a large amount of evaporation. As the water vapor rises, it condenses to form huge clouds. In so doing, it releases large amounts of heat into the atmosphere. This additional heat fuels the developing thunderstorms. Meteorologists watch for these thunderstorms on satellite pictures. An area of thunderstorms that appears to be developing creates the stage of a *tropical cyclone* called a *tropical disturbance.* As the thunderstorms join together

The Stages of Tropical Cyclones

Tropical disturbance Maximum sustained winds are less than 23 miles (37 km) per hour.

Tropical depression Maximum sustained winds are 23–38 miles (37–61 km) per hour. Tropical depressions are given numbers.

Tropical storm Maximum sustained winds are 39–73 miles (63–117 km) per hour. Tropical storms are given names.

Hurricane Maximum sustained winds are greater than 74 miles (119 km) per hour.

and the system increases to several miles in diameter, it begins to spin, the air pressure drops, and the winds increase. Meteorologists call this stage of a tropical cyclone a *tropical depression*. If the atmospheric conditions are right, higher pressure develops above the depression, and the air starts to flow out the top. This causes the warm air near the ocean surface to be pulled upward—like smoke up a chimney. The rising, warm, moist air creates more clouds, which release more heat, which contributes to more outflow. The system gets stronger. Once the winds top 74 miles (119 km) per hour, it is a hurricane, as shown in the "Stages of Tropical Cyclones" sidebar above.

Hurricanes are called *typhoons* in the West Pacific Ocean, *willy-willies* in Australia, and *cyclones* in the Indian Ocean. The hurricanes that are most likely to affect the continental United States form in the North Atlantic Ocean, the Caribbean Sea, and the Gulf of Mexico. Tropical storms and hurricanes that form in the early part of the hurricane season (June and July) tend to occur in the southern Gulf of Mexico or the southwestern Caribbean Sea, because the shallow water warms up more quickly than the deeper ocean water. However, as the summer progresses, the tropical waters of the Atlantic become very warm—over 84°F (29°C) in August and September—and the high ocean surface temperatures spread eastward. Tropical storms and hurricanes that develop in the late summer tend to develop off the coast of Africa, near the Cape Verde Islands. Therefore, late summer hurricanes are sometimes called Cape Verde storms.

Well-developed hurricanes have a clear central *eye* 5–50 miles (8–80 km) across, surrounded by the tall, massive thunderstorms of the *eye wall,* which can climb to a height of 8.7 miles (14 km). (Imagine a doughnut—the hole in the middle is the eye and the cake is the eye wall.) There is no rain and almost no wind in the eye. The eye wall contains the heaviest rains and the strongest winds. As the strong thunderstorms of the eye wall pull in yet more moist air, spiral bands of thunderstorms hundreds of miles long connect to the eye wall and turn like a pinwheel. As the hurricane comes ashore, the spiral bands move over the land, producing gusty winds and heavy rain showers.

A hurricane can move over small islands without ever losing its energy source—the warm ocean water. However, once the storm moves over a continent, it is cut off from its energy source and starts to fall apart. Before it completely dies, its clouds drop all their accumulated moisture, so heavy rains and flooding may result even as the winds weaken.

One might think that the high winds, heavy rains, and tornadoes that sometimes appear from the thunderstorms in a hurricane's eye wall would produce its greatest dangers. They do not. The most dangerous result of a hurricane is the storm surge, which can crush homes and small multistory buildings. Getting out of the way of the storm surge is impossible. Once a person sees it coming, it is too late to escape. If the storm surge arrives at the same time as high tide, the arriving water will be at its maximum possible height and can extend many miles inland over flat coastal terrain. The water can completely cover any islands that are in the way.

Hurricanes are rated from 1 to 5 on a scale called the *Saffir-Simpson hurricane scale,* shown in the "Saffir-Simpson Hurricane Scale" sidebar on page 6. The scale, developed by structural engineer Herbert S. Saffir and tropical meteorologist Robert Simpson (who was the director of the National Hurricane Center), classifies hurricanes by their intensity. Emergency planners use the scale to estimate the level of damage and flooding that might occur from a hurricane. The total amount of damage caused by hurricanes depends on two factors: their strength and where they come ashore.

Environmental Changes

Wherever hurricanes come ashore, they change the existing natural environment. The extent of the change depends on the storm's strength and the area's ecology. If, for example, the hurricane comes ashore in an area already saturated by heavy rains and drops another 2 feet (0.6 m) of rain, the floods that result could wipe out any land animals living there. If the storm surge is extremely high and the land is extremely flat and poorly drained, the saltwater could remain for many days and poison the land, killing the plants that live there.

Hurricanes can also modify offshore areas. Large waves whipped up by heavy winds can scrape the ocean bottom as the water gets shallower toward land. Coral, sponges, and the marine animals that live among them may be killed. Without coral *reefs* to attract fish, it may take many years before the fish return.

When a less intense hurricane strikes an environment that can stand up to high winds and seas, it does relatively little damage. However, if the hurricane is extremely strong and the area that it hits has an *ecosystem* that is sensitive to any serious change in the weather, it may be many years before native plants and animals return.

The Saffir-Simpson Hurricane Scale

Category	Wind speed
1	74–95 mph (119–153 km/hr, 64–82 knots)
	Unanchored mobile homes, trees, and shrubs will be damaged, but most buildings will not. The low storm surge of 4–5 feet (1.2–1.5 m) may cause some coastal flooding and pier damage.
2	96–110 mph (154–177 km/hr, 83–95 knots)
	More serious damage is done to mobile homes, trees, and shrubs. Windows, doors, and roofs of buildings will experience some damage. A higher storm surge of 6–8 feet (1.8–2.4 m) will flood low-lying escape routes two to four hours before the hurricane arrives. The storm surge will damage piers.
3	111–130 mph (178–209 km/hr, 96–113 knots)
	Mobile homes are destroyed. Trees are blown down. Small buildings (including homes) experience some structural damage. The storm surge of 9–12 feet (2.7–3.6 m) cuts off escape routes three to five hours before the hurricane center arrives and destroys small structures near the coast. If the land is flat—5 feet (1.5 m) or less above sea level—the water may flood inland up to 8 miles (12.9 km). Evacuations are probably required.
4	131–155 mph (210–249 km/hr, 114–135 knots)
	Mobile homes are completely destroyed. Roofs are blown off some small buildings, with much damage to doors and windows. Trees and signs are blown down. The storm surge of 13–18 feet (4–5.5 m) cuts off evacuation routes three to five hours before the hurricane's center arrives. If the land elevation is below 10 feet (3 m), floodwaters may spread 6 miles (9.6 km). Evacuations are necessary.
5	Greater than 155 mph (249 km/hr, 135 knots)
	Mobile homes and some small structures are completely destroyed. Roofs fail completely on many homes and industrial buildings. All trees and signs are blown down, and there is massive failure of windows and doors. The storm surge of over 18 feet (5.5 m) arrives three to five hours before the hurricane's center. It will damage structures within 1,500 feet (457 m) of the shoreline and cut off escape routes. Massive evacuations may be required.

Impact on Humans

As with the environment, how much damage a hurricane inflicts on the population depends on how many people live in the area, how they decided to develop land and build structures there, and how well prepared they are. If a weak hurricane comes ashore in an area with few people—and they have all left in advance of the storm—there will probably be no deaths. However, if a strong hurricane comes ashore in an area where hundreds of thousands of people live very close together, the potential for large loss of life is high.

Homes built very close to the ocean will experience greater damage than those built inland, no matter how well built they are. Homes, office buildings, and factories built to withstand hurricane-force winds survive better and with less damage than buildings (such as mobile homes) that are easily torn apart by high winds. However, almost no building can withstand a direct hit by a category 5 hurricane and emerge with no damage.

Even waves from category 3 hurricanes can uplift motor vehicles and cause property damage to structures that are not heavy or well anchored. (Photo courtesy of National Oceanic and Atmospheric Administration/Department of Commerce)

Hurricane winds can also blow trees across roads, and flood-waters can cover streets. Hurricanes can destroy electricity grids, leaving affected areas without power. With the power out and too much dirty water entering sanitation systems, clean water may be unavailable for several days to several weeks. Dirty water can carry serious diseases such as cholera and typhoid and can provide a home for mosquitoes that can themselves carry disease.

Although there is no possible way to protect all property from damage, it is possible to prevent loss of life by evacuating people away from the path of a hurricane before it arrives. However, it is almost impossible to evacuate everyone from very large coastal cities because there are not enough roads leading out to safer areas. Therefore, emergency planners need to develop plans to move people to safety in well-made buildings within the city that will keep them out of high water.

Deadly Hurricanes

On average, 5.7 hurricanes develop during each Atlantic Ocean hurricane season. Sometimes there are more, and sometimes fewer. Sometimes the hurricanes are weak—and sometimes they are strong. Several strong hurricanes in the early part of the 20th century in the United States left thousands of people dead. The largest tropical system in the 20th century killed between 300,000 and 500,000 people in Bangladesh.

Before weather satellites appeared in the 1960s, people were often caught by surprise when hurricanes came ashore in the United States. Depending on a storm's track, people in the Caribbean could send a warning to U.S. meteorologists—but only if their own telegraph equipment was not damaged by the storm. Ships' captains would also send in reports of high winds and seas that might indicate the arrival of a hurricane. However, there was really no way to predict where a hurricane would come ashore, and people did not have time to prepare.

The most deadly weather disaster in U.S. history was the Galveston hurricane of 1900, which struck Cuba as a tropical storm on September 3, 1900, and then became stronger as it passed over the Gulf of Mexico. As a category 4 hurricane, it struck Galveston Island, Texas, with storm tides (the storm surge combined with astronomical high tides) of 8–15 feet (2.4–4.6 m) that swamped the island and the surrounding Texas coastline. Most of the 6,000 to 12,000 deaths were due to drowning in the high, churning water. So many people were washed out to sea that an exact death count was never finalized. After the storm, city leaders built large seawalls to keep out hurricane-driven water. So far, the seawalls have kept Galveston's residents safe from high water.

The Great Miami Hurricane of 1926 caught the residents of Miami, Florida, by surprise. Although meteorologists knew that a tropical system was developing, they did not have solid information on its whereabouts until just after midnight on September 18, when they put out a warning—too late. The category 4 hurricane made a direct hit on Miami a few hours later, bringing winds over 120 miles (193 km) per hour and a storm surge of almost 15 feet (4.6 m). The hurricane continued across the Gulf of Mexico until it hit Pensacola, Florida, where it destroyed virtually every structure on Pensacola Bay. At least 373 people died and over 6,000 were injured. More than 800 people were listed as missing. The Great Miami Hurricane ended a period of rapid economic growth in South Florida. Because of the increased number of buildings in the area now, a similar storm today would cause more than $90 billion in damage.

The most intense hurricane ever to hit the United States came ashore as the Florida Keys Labor Day hurricane of 1935. This hurricane was first detected just east of the Bahamas on August 29. By September 2, when it hit the Florida Keys, it was a category 5 hurricane. The high wind and high water killed over 400 people in the Keys and caused an estimated $6 million in damage.

The Galveston hurricane of 1900 is considered the most deadly weather disaster in U.S. history. Huge waves swamped the island, destroying virtually everyone and everything in their path. (Photo courtesy of Associated Press)

Not all major hurricanes hit Florida and the gulf coast states. In 1938 the New England hurricane traveled parallel to the Atlantic coast and took aim at New York and Connecticut. Arriving as a category 3 storm on September 21, it packed winds over 120 miles (193 km) per hour and a storm surge of 10–12 feet (3–3.6 m). Heavy rains fell, and river flooding was widespread. More than five hundred people died in the New England hurricane, and damage was estimated at $308 million.

Unlike the hurricanes discussed above, which all started in the Atlantic Ocean, Hurricane Camille formed west of the Cayman Islands in the Caribbean Sea on August 14, 1969. Just one day later, it was a category 3 hurricane. Late on August 17, it arrived on the Mississippi coast as a category 5 hurricane. Camille, the second-most intense hurricane to hit the United States, destroyed all the wind-measuring equipment in the area, so no one will ever know how fast the wind was blowing. However, meteorologists estimate that winds near the coast were about 200 miles (322 km) per hour. The storm surge of 24.6 feet (7.5 m) came ashore at Pass Christian, Mississippi, wiping out most of this low-lying town.

As Camille moved inland, it weakened to become a tropical depression. When it passed over Virginia, Camille dropped 12–20 inches (30.5–51 cm) of rain within five hours. The resulting flash floods caused tremendous damage and contributed to the deaths of 113 people. Another 143 people died as a result of the hurricane itself, and $1.4 billion of property was destroyed. Many of those who died in Mississippi had ignored evacuation warnings and remained in their homes.

Devastating hurricanes have hit a number of other countries around the world—some causing almost unimaginable numbers of deaths. The Bangladesh Cyclone of November 1970 developed in the Indian Ocean. When this system hit the very flat, low-lying Bangladesh coast, it submerged the land with a tremendous storm surge that killed between 300,000 and 500,000 people and an equally large number of animals. The water had no place to drain off, so the land was flooded. Without a clean water supply, waterborne diseases increased the death toll.

Japan is also a target for hurricanes. Typhoon Vera in 1959 was the largest weather disaster in Japanese history. Almost 5,000 people died and 1.5 million people were left homeless. The resulting damage to roads, bridges, and communications systems from Vera's wind, floods, and landslides severely crippled Japan's economy.

Hurricane Mitch hit Honduras in the western Caribbean on October 29, 1998. Although it had been a category 5 hurricane, Mitch had weakened to a category 1 by the time it came ashore in Honduras. However, it dropped large amounts of rain in Honduras, Nicaragua, Guatemala, and El Salvador. The water raced down steep hillsides, causing massive flooding and landslides that killed at least 9,000 people and left another 9,000 missing. Mitch regained strength in the Gulf of Mexico and sped toward South Florida, where it came ashore as a tropical storm on November 5. Two fishermen died in the Florida Keys, and Mitch caused $40 million in property damage in South Florida.

Isabel, the first category 5 Atlantic hurricane since Mitch, had weakened to a category 2 before it slammed into the Outer Banks of North Carolina on September 18, 2003. Continuing into Virginia, Isabel's heavy rains added water to soil already soaked by earlier rainstorms. When the hurricane-force winds blew in, the soggy ground was not able to hold large trees, which fell across power lines in great numbers. Approximately 1.8 million people were left without power. Isabel left 40 people dead and caused almost $1 billion in damage.

In 2004 Florida matched a record previously set by Texas in 1886 when four hurricanes struck the state between the middle of August and the end of September. Category 4 Charley was the

In November 1998, the Mercado San Isidro, a thriving market in Tegucigalpa, Honduras, was destroyed by flooding from Hurricane Mitch. Many people who lost their jobs or places of business faced hardship for months to come. (Photo courtesy of Associated Press)

first to strike when it plowed into Punta Gorda, Florida, with winds of 145 miles (233 kilometers) per hour on August 13.

The next system, Frances, was only a category 2 storm, but it was three times larger than Charley and moved much more slowly, delivering a lot of rain. Frances made landfall on September 5 approximately 35 miles (56 km) north of West Palm Beach. Some nearby areas received over 10 inches (25 cm) of rain within a couple of days.

Ivan, which ripped up the islands of Granada, Jamaica, Cuba, and the Caymans during its trip through the Caribbean as an off-and-on category 5 storm, struck near Mobile, Alabama, as a category 3 storm on September 16. The worst of the winds hit Pensacola, Florida—a few miles to the east. Tornadoes, heavy rain, and strong winds caused massive damage in the Florida Panhandle. "Ivan the Terrible" later looped back into the Gulf of Mexico as a tropical storm and came ashore again in Louisiana.

Florida residents could not believe it when Jeanne, a hurricane that had "died" and come back to life in the warm Atlantic waters, circled back around, came ashore on September 26, and followed almost the exact same path as Frances. Utilities had not yet been restored from the earlier storms when Jeanne added several inches of rain to the misery. However, the people of Haiti bore the main brunt of Jeanne's fury. The rainfall from Jeanne washed down hillsides and swept through the town of Gonaives. Over 2,000 people were known to be dead, and the total may exceed 3,000. When all of the damage is added up, the 2004 hurricane season may be the most costly on record.

Hurricanes are always part of a year's weather events. The number of deaths and the amount of damage are directly related to the environment (flat or mountainous, populated or not) that the hurricane encounters and to the preparation of governments and residents of the area. This book will now tell the story of the hurricane that caused a record amount of economic devastation in the United States—the story of Andrew.

CHAPTER 2

Hurricane Andrew Comes Ashore

This aerial photograph taken on September 4, 1992, shows the complete devastation wrought on the city of Florida City, Florida, by Hurricane Andrew. (Photo courtesy of Associated Press)

Often, a hurricane leaves its tropical birthplace and comes to land in the *subtropics*—the region just slightly farther from the equator than the tropics. Andrew's three targets—the Bahamas, South Florida, and south-central Louisiana—all lie within the subtropics. All three have similar landforms—they are close to the ocean and they have very low elevations. The highest point in the Bahamas, for example, is only 206 feet (62.8 m) above sea level. Marshes and *swamps* that actually lie below sea level are characteristic of parts of southern Florida and Louisiana.

The Bahamas is a group of over 700 islands scattered across 100,000 square miles (259,000 km²) of the Atlantic Ocean just

east of Florida. Although the island chain extends eastward for 750 miles (1,210 km), all of the islands put together would fit into the state of Connecticut with space left over. When Andrew hit in 1992, about 255,000 people lived in the Bahamas, 80 percent of them on just two islands: Grand Bahama and New Providence. Tourism provides over half the economic base for the Bahamas, with banking and related financial services also providing important income to the country. The rocky outcrops are not suitable for farming, and less than 0.4 percent of the land area is under cultivation. Raising poultry is a significant part of the economy—there are three times as many chickens as people living in the Bahamas. However, over 85 percent of the food is imported.

South Florida—the only part of the state affected by Andrew—is also heavily dependent on tourism. Andrew came ashore in Dade County, which extends from just north of Miami south to the Florida Keys. While Miami is a glittering, vibrant, prosperous city, the southern part of Dade County is an economically depressed area. Although Homestead Air Force Base provided thousands of middle-class jobs, southern Dade is also home to numerous immigrants from the Caribbean, Mexico, and Central America who work as migrant laborers, following the crops as they ripen and need to be picked. When Andrew took aim at Dade County, 2 million people were in its path.

Southern Louisiana is the lowest lying of all of Andrew's targets. The city of New Orleans actually lies below sea level, protected by an elaborate system of *levees*—some of which will fail during strong hurricanes and major floods—and pumps that keep the water from the Gulf of Mexico, the Mississippi River, Lake Pontchartrain, and Lake Borgne away from downtown. Since most of the state's residents live in New Orleans and its surrounding suburbs, the rest of southern Louisiana is sparsely populated swampland. The area is important for fisheries and as the land base for the thriving petroleum industry in the Gulf of Mexico.

University of Florida engineering professor Kurt Gurley demonstrates an experiment for U.S. senator Bob Graham (left). The test simulates the force of large flying objects in a category 4 hurricane. New building codes for schools in Florida state that the structures must be able to withstand flying objects in a category 3 hurricane. (Photo courtesy of Associated Press)

Why Study Andrew?

Andrew was the most expensive natural disaster in U.S. history. Andrew was also unique for a variety of other reasons—some scientific and some political. As a category 5 hurricane (it was upgraded from category 4 to category 5 in 2003 after further data analysis), Andrew could have caused even more widespread damage than it did. However, unlike most powerful hurricanes, Andrew was extremely compact: its *center* (its eye and surrounding eye wall) was only 25 miles (40 km) in diameter. Therefore, the path of destruction was limited to an extremely tight area matching the wall clouds that surrounded its eye. Most hurricanes—even weaker ones—tend to have larger eyes and eye walls, and strong convective bands that can cause considerable damage over a swath more than 62 miles (100 km) wide.

Furthermore, considering the total physical destruction inflicted by Andrew, one would expect that the corresponding death and injury toll would have been much higher. Weaker storms than Andrew have caused thousands of deaths. However, accurate forecasts and the heeding of evacuation orders prevented a large loss of life. Andrew took the lives of 15 people in Florida during the storm itself, and most of those deaths would have been prevented if those people had evacuated. After the storm passed, 29 more Floridians died while cleaning up the debris.

Andrew was also unique because of the wide-ranging environmental changes that resulted. From coral reefs to ecologically sensitive swamps to fragile *barrier islands,* Andrew affected a variety of landforms both offshore and on land. In addition, it inflicted considerable damage on agricultural land and fisheries.

Finally, Andrew exposed serious deficiencies in *building codes* and enforcement of those codes that would have prevented some building damage. Problems with recovery efforts underscored the requirement for careful coordination between federal, state, and local government agencies to address the aftermath of catastrophic events. This storm also made clear that when a massive hurricane hits a high-population area, no relief effort—no matter how well organized and executed—will alleviate the suffering of its victims quickly.

The Birth of Andrew

Hurricane Andrew started as a *tropical wave*—a disturbed area of low-pressure air—that moved across the west coast of Africa and into the tropical North Atlantic Ocean on August 14, 1992. No one knew that this small tropical wave would turn into the first hurricane of the 1992 season—much less that it would be such a spectacular system. Despite its unimpressive appearance, the tropical meteorology experts at the National Hurricane Center (NHC) in Miami started to track this new system. They noted

Max Mayfield, director of the National Hurricane Center in Miami, Florida, announces on August 21, 2002, that Hurricane Andrew had gone from a category 4 storm to a category 5 storm. The hurricane had gained strength over the warm waters of the southwestern Atlantic. (Photo courtesy of Associated Press)

that convective clouds were starting to rotate about a center. Within two more days, narrow, spiral-shaped bands of clouds began to rotate around this same center. The tropical wave became a tropical depression with winds of 29 miles (46.6 km) per hour (25 knots). Less than a day later, on August 17, at 8:00 A.M. Eastern Daylight Time (EDT), the forecasters upgraded the depression to a tropical storm and named it Andrew. Andrew's maximum wind speed at this point was 40 miles (64.4 km) per hour (35 knots).

Over the next three days, a very large high-pressure system located over the eastern Atlantic steered Andrew westward. Andrew's winds remained the same over the next three days, ranging from 46–52 miles (74–83.7 km) per hour (40–45 knots). The tropical storm's central pressure, which meteorologists expected to be low, was actually a high 29.97 inches of mercury

(1015 millibars). Meteorologists measure air pressure—the force of air pushing down on Earth—in either inches of mercury or millibars. On average, the air pressure on a clear, warm day is about 29.53 inches of mercury (1,000 millibars).

On August 21, significant changes in the atmosphere began to affect Andrew. The upper-level pattern—which allowed the air rising up through the convective cells to flow out—strengthened Andrew. A large high-pressure system formed near the coast of the southeastern United States and then extended across the southwestern Atlantic so that it was just north of Andrew. This high-pressure ridge forced Andrew to track directly west. The very warm water under Andrew provided the storm with a fresh energy supply. Consequently, the storm strengthened rapidly. By the morning of August 22, Andrew had become the first Atlantic hurricane of 1992, with winds of 80 miles (129 km) per hour (70 knots). Andrew was also the first hurricane in two years to have started out as a tropical wave just off the African coastline.

Andrew continued to strengthen. Within 36 hours of reaching hurricane strength, Andrew's Saffir-Simpson classification was at the border between category 4 and category 5. As the high-pressure area held steady north of Andrew, the hurricane continued on its westerly path. The storm was ready to pay its first call—to the Bahamas.

The Bahamas

Andrew's first target was the Bahamas. The NHC issued the first hurricane watch at 11:00 A.M. (EDT) on August 22, for the northwest Bahamas, about 30 hours before Andrew hit. Six hours later—24 hours before Andrew hit—the NHC issued the first hurricane warning. The difference between a hurricane watch and a hurricane warning is highlighted in the "Watch or Warning?" sidebar on page 20. The Bahamians, accustomed to damage from hurricane winds and storm surges, heeded the

Watch or Warning?

A *hurricane watch* advises residents to get ready—a hurricane could arrive in 36 hours. They should check their hurricane plans, get non-perishable food, extra bottled water, and batteries for radios and flashlights, and make arrangements for elderly family members, children, and pets to be in a safe place.

A *hurricane warning* advises residents that winds in excess of 74 miles (119 km) per hour will arrive at their location in 24 hours or less. They should board up their windows, move objects that are not tied down into safe places, secure their boats, and get to a safe place themselves.

warnings and headed for shelters. Some vacationers were picked up on a ship and transported to Florida, as the sidebar "An Exciting Vacation?" on page 22 relates.

Andrew reached its peak strength just before striking the island of Eleuthera. When it hit at about 6:00 P.M. (EDT), the category 4 hurricane was packing winds of 150 miles (241 km) per hour. However, that wind speed was based on an analysis of satellite pictures—the anemometer (an instrument for measuring wind speed) on Eleuthera could only measure up to 120 miles (193 km) per hour. Three hours later, Andrew hit New Providence Island in the southern Berry Islands. The storm surge that slammed into the islands was between 16 and 23 feet (4.9 and 7 m) high and caused extensive flooding. Damage on New Providence Island was minimal, although one death was reported. Eleuthera had been hit harder: five schools and 800 homes were damaged, 1,700 people were left homeless, and three people died. The hurricane severely damaged the island's water, sanitation, telecommunications, airport, and *marinas*. Telephone communications remained out for almost a week after Andrew passed through. Agricultural and fishing losses were also significant. Andrew's short visit to the Bahamas caused a total of $250 million in property damage to the islands.

South Florida

Although there was no certainty that Andrew would intensify—much less actually strike Florida—officials of the South Florida Water Management District started to lower the water levels in several lakes in the Upper Kissimmee Valley on Thursday, August 20, as a precaution. Heavy rains had already raised lake levels at or above flood stage, and officials did not want to take a chance of drenching rains from Andrew sending water into populated areas. On August 21, as Andrew gained strength, Florida put its emergency response officials on standby alert. As NHC Deputy Director Jerry Jarrell put it, "All along the Florida coast, later in the weekend, people need to be alert for something to happen." Noting that Andrew was a "weird duck," Jarrell announced that there was a one in three chance that Andrew would turn north and miss Florida. However, there were no guarantees. People needed to prepare. The "Preparing for Hurricanes" sidebar on page 24 tells how to get ready for a hurricane.

Acting on the information from the NHC, Broward and Palm Beach County emergency directors requested their key employees to stay near their phones on Sunday, August 23—just in case. Similarly, Red Cross disaster directors advised their shelter coordinators to get ready. With 1.3 million people living in flood-prone areas, they knew it would take 21 hours to evacuate Broward in a minor hurricane. If Andrew turned into a major hurricane, more people would have to leave, and it would take longer. As these officials prepared, Andrew was heading straight for Florida. However, as night fell on Friday evening, there was no panic. Almost no one was stocking up on supplies.

On Saturday morning, August 22, the NHC advised people to get ready. Andrew, still a tropical storm, was 900 miles (1,448 km) east of Florida. Jarrell, keeping a close eye on the storm, realized that this storm could become dangerous if it came ashore in Florida with winds over 90 miles (145 km) per hour. "It's not to say that is going to cream South Florida," Jarrell admitted, "but it's out there and it's headed in this general direction. Look around and see what you can do before the last minute gets here." By 5:00 P.M. (EDT), Andrew was a hurricane growing in strength 615 miles (989 km) east of Miami. The hurricane specialists at the

An Exciting Vacation?

Because the Bahamas is a tourist destination, hundreds of vacationers found themselves caught on the islands with Andrew bearing down on them. The cruise ship *Sea Escape* sailed from Fort Lauderdale, Florida, to Freeport in the Bahamas just before Andrew's arrival on Sunday, August 23, and picked up 1,400 panicked passengers. They arrived later in the day in Port Everglades, Florida—24 hours before Andrew hit Florida.

NHC could not yet pinpoint where the storm would strike—everyone along the south coast of Florida had to be prepared. Broward and Palm Beach counties activated their emergency stations, and the Red Cross set up shelters and called in volunteers. Radio and television stations prepared to stay on the air to provide much-needed information.

Sunday arrived with a hurricane watch covering the east coast of Florida south of Vero Beach. By noon, that had been upgraded to a hurricane warning. Andrew would arrive in less than 24 hours. Hurricane specialist Lixion Avila clearly spelled out the severity of the situation: "The eye is definitely going to hit somewhere in South Florida. Wherever the eye hits will be leveled. This is going to be the worst. There is no chance that this would not hit us." (Although the hurricane's eye is calm, the storm's strongest winds are right around it. The highest winds strike just before and after the eye passes over.)

A few residents decided that they would ride out the storm in their homes, but most of the 1.2 million people in the evacuation zone decided to leave. They crowded grocery stores for food, ATMs for cash, gas stations to fill the tanks of their cars, and hardware stores for sheets of plywood to cover their windows. Those precautions taken, they got on the Florida turnpike and headed north to safety. Some decided to seek refuge in local shelters. Police drove down the streets broadcasting evacuation orders, and they knocked on doors of high-rise apartment buildings, urging people to seek safety in shelters.

Roaring like a speeding freight train, Andrew came ashore as a category 5 hurricane around 5:00 A.M. (EDT), on Monday, August 24, directly over Homestead Air Force Base. Meteorologists estimated that Andrew's maximum *sustained winds* were more than 145 miles (233 km) per hour. The air force's anemometer "pegged" (the indicator stopped working) at 145 miles per hour. At the NHC near Miami, the anemometer recorded 164 miles (264 km) per hour before it was destroyed. Unofficial reports of *funnel clouds* (tornado-type clouds that do not touch the ground) came in from Glades, Collier, and Highland counties.

Andrew's forward motion of 18 miles (29 km) per hour was sufficiently fast to keep precipitation amounts relatively low for a hurricane. A rain gauge in Broward County recorded 7.79 inches (19.79 cm) and one in Dade County showed 7.41 inches (18.82 cm). The storm tide was 16.9 feet (5.1 m) in Biscayne Bay—a local maximum that caused flooding.

Most damage in Florida was caused by the wind, and not by the storm surge, which is unusual for many hurricanes. Within the 24.8-mile (40-km) diameter of the hurricane's moving center, 25,524 homes were destroyed, 101,241 were damaged, and 250,000 people were left homeless. Almost all the mobile homes in the area were destroyed—90 percent of all mobile homes in Dade County and 99 percent of all mobile homes in the city of Homestead. Fifteen people died as a direct result of the storm (most hit by flying or falling debris), while 14 died of stress-induced heart attacks during the hurricane. Fifteen more died after the hurricane had passed. Some of these people died when they were cleaning debris in their upper-floor apartments and fell out of windows. Others had trees fall on them. Total financial losses were $25 billion.

Louisiana

Zipping out of Florida, a slightly weakened Andrew moved out over the warm waters of the Gulf of Mexico. At 5:00 P.M. (EDT), on August 24, the NHC issued a hurricane warning for the gulf coast between Pascagoula, Mississippi, and Vermilion Bay, Louisiana. By

Preparing for Hurricanes

Once a hurricane arrives, it is too late to get ready. People who live in hurricane-prone areas know that they need to take certain steps before the hurricane arrives. Typically, they buy enough nonperishable (canned or boxed) food for themselves and their pets for a week or two and either fill containers with fresh, clean water or purchase bottled water. They also stock up on prescription medications, buy batteries for flashlights and radios, fill their cars and trucks with gasoline, and get some cash. To prepare their homes, they cover their windows with sheets of plywood to prevent breakage and put away lawn chairs and other loose objects in the yard. Then they map out their possible evacuation route and make sure that they have a safe place to go.

the following morning, Andrew's next landing site had been narrowed down to between Vermilion Bay and Port Arthur, Texas. Louisiana governor Edwin Edwards declared a state of emergency and asked that his state be declared a disaster area even before Andrew struck land. Over 2 million people in southern Mississippi, Louisiana, and Texas were asked to evacuate. At 4:30 A.M. (EDT) on Wednesday, August 26, Andrew came ashore in the marshy coastal area near Point Chevreuil, Louisiana, some 20 miles (32.2 km) west-southwest of Morgan City. With winds of 105 miles (169 km) per hour, Andrew was now a category 3 hurricane.

In contrast to Andrew's performance in Florida, the storm spawned a number of tornadoes in Louisiana before its formal arrival. Two people died and 32 people were injured in Laplace, Louisiana, when a tornado touched down. Five other Louisiana parishes (counties) reported damage that officials suspected was caused by tornadoes. Precipitation was also more severe in Louisiana. Andrew was moving slower and therefore had the opportunity to drop more water—a maximum of 11.92 inches (30.28 cm) at Hammond, Louisiana. The combination of extensive rainfall and a storm tide of at least 8 feet (2.4 m) caused flooding from Lake Borgne to Vermilion Bay.

Andrew destroyed approximately 2,000 homes and 1,000 businesses in Terrebonne Parish when it came ashore. Eight deaths were directly attributed to the storm, and another nine deaths occurred during the recovery effort. The total damage in

Louisiana cost $1 billion. Petroleum drilling sites out in the Gulf of Mexico suffered another $500 million in damage.

The remains of Andrew sped north and east out of Louisiana and headed toward Virginia, dropping rain along the way. On August 28, two days after coming ashore in Louisiana, what had been Andrew joined up with a *frontal system* off the coast of Virginia and continued out into the Atlantic Ocean.

Adding Up the Cost

Andrew made direct hits on three different population centers, causing extensive damage at each. The impact on people was immediate—houses were destroyed, electric lines were blown over or pulled down by falling trees, water supplies were left unsafe to drink, and businesses were unable to continue. While electricity and water were restored within a few weeks, it took longer to clean up the debris and for life to return to normal. In all, Andrew caused $26.75 billion in damage, and a total of 65 people were killed, directly or indirectly, as a result of this storm.

CHAPTER 3

Stunned by Destruction

Janny Vancedarfield was left homeless after Hurricane Andrew destroyed his house in Florida City, Florida. Hundreds of people were left in similar circumstances when the storm passed through this town. (Photo courtesy of Associated Press)

Many people compared the destruction left by Andrew to the damage resulting from a nuclear bomb explosion. After Andrew's center passed over Homestead, Florida, almost nothing was left standing. Those who stayed in their homes to ride out the storm—and lived—told harrowing tales of their experience.

Remaining in her home outside the eye of the hurricane, Theresa Sandalson of Miami Beach listened in horror as Andrew whistled past. "It was," she told the *Washington Post*, "the most terri-

fying moment of my life. I wanted to scream, the wind was so loud. I didn't have anywhere to go." Throughout South Florida people who had never experienced the fury of a hurricane took refuge in interior bathrooms or closets—anywhere that they could protect themselves from debris flying through broken windows.

A family living in West Kendall, Florida, decided to stay in their wood-frame house. At first, they were just concerned about their landscaping—the carefully planted trees, shrubs, and flowers that graced their yard. Then their house blew apart. As the wind roared around them, they huddled together in an interior bathroom and prayed for their survival. When the roaring stopped, they looked out to see that the rest of their house was gone.

Other survivors of Andrew described leaning against bathroom doors with their feet braced against bathtubs to keep the wind and rain from coming in. People pulled mattresses over themselves for protection from falling beams. All agreed that they would never, ever try to ride out a hurricane—any hurricane—again. Another tale of survival is related in the "Safety Fish?" sidebar above.

While some people decided to remain in their homes, over 1 million others decided that the risk was too great. However, most Floridians who left their homes for shelters did not plan on a long stay. Typical among these families were those from the Cutler Ridge area south of Miami. Planning to stay just for the night, they took their pillows and blankets with them to the local shelter on Sunday evening before Andrew was due to arrive. They figured that Andrew would blow through during the night and early the

Safety Fish?

The Mullins family owned a fish store just south of Miami. Since the store was built of concrete blocks, they thought that they would be safe there during Hurricane Andrew. Fourteen members of their extended clan gathered inside the store to wait out Andrew's passage. As the hurricane bore down on them, the walls shook, the roof blew off, and rainwater poured through the ceiling. Worried that the shaking walls might collapse on them, they retreated to the 8-foot by 8-foot (2.4-m by 2.4-m) fish locker and stayed there until it was safe to venture out for a look around. Said one family member, "We thought we were going to die."

next morning, and then they could just go home in the afternoon. They were wrong. After a night of howling winds and pounding rain, there were no homes left—just piles of rubble. The Cutler Ridge refugees were shuttled to new shelters that could provide them with food, water, electricity, and working sanitation systems.

Louisiana and Texas residents did not need much encouragement to evacuate after seeing television reports of the devastation inflicted by Andrew in Florida. (More on the media coverage of the hurricane is related in the "Media Coverage of Andrew" sidebar on page 30.) As one resident put it, "I'd rather stay home, but I've got grandkids, and you never know what can happen." Most shelters—sturdy concrete block buildings with small, shatterproof windows—lacked food, and people did not bring much with them, expecting a short stay. However, most considered being a little hungry a better alternative to being washed away by Andrew.

Government Response

All levels of government had tried to prepare before Andrew arrived, but none was ready for the hurricane's devastation. As relief efforts began, two immediate concerns were safety and law enforcement. With windows and doors smashed by the storm, looting of businesses and homes was a serious problem. Local police and National Guard troops enforced a curfew from 7:00 P.M. to 7:00 A.M. (EDT) to keep people off the streets.

Dade County officials were overwhelmed not only by the storm's destruction, but also by the amount of food, water, and fuel that they needed to distribute to desperate people. Even though there was immediate need, poor coordination between agencies and blocked transportation routes kept local officials from opening distribution centers until three days after Andrew struck. Meanwhile, fire and rescue teams, joined by National Guard troops, fanned out to look for those killed or injured in rural areas that were cut off from major transportation routes.

Florida governor Lawton Chiles could not believe what he saw in southern Dade County. "It is hard to come up with a word to describe it," he said. "If you look at Homestead, it looks like an atomic bomb went off over it and flattened it." Emergency equipment was ready to go, but the turnpikes were jammed with people attempting to drive home. Once the equipment reached turnpike off-ramps, drivers were faced with so much debris that it was difficult to determine where they were or how to find their destinations. Clearly, outside help was needed, and it came from the federal government.

President George H.W. Bush, touring South Miami, announced that the federal government would do "everything possible to help," including sending in troops if Florida's leaders requested them. He declared Dade, Broward, and Monroe counties federal disaster areas, thus making them eligible for government aid.

However, there were problems with the federal response. The agency responsible for federal disaster relief—the Federal Emergency Management Agency (FEMA)—was totally unprepared. Staffed by political appointees with no experience in emergency preparedness or relief activities, FEMA did not set up its first field disaster office until three days after Andrew's arrival. The offices that were set up were understaffed, and workers had little money to give out as emergency loans. FEMA employees demanded more financial and property documentation from homeless Floridians than they were able to provide. People seeking assistance were often handed cards with toll-free numbers on them and told to call for help—except that the telephone system no longer worked. Adding to the confusion, some centers were placed in low-population areas that could not be reached because of debris in the roads. At those centers, FEMA workers had almost nothing to do. FEMA also promised to bring in 2,800 trailers as emergency housing, but with 100,000 homeless, these trailers would be able to meet the needs of only a handful of people.

Media Coverage of Andrew

The massive devastation caused by Andrew was a magnet for the media—major television networks and newspapers converged on Florida to beam photos of flattened buildings and stories of survivors around the nation and the world. When reporters realized that promised relief efforts were not appearing, the stories of government failure were featured on the evening news and on the front pages of major newspapers like the *New York Times* and the *Washington Post*. The inability of the Federal Emergency Management Agency (FEMA) to address the basic needs of Floridians brought harsh criticism and forced the federal government to provide military troops and equipment to help. The stories also touched the hearts of the nation, and funds poured in to relief organizations providing shelter, food, and water to the hard-hit residents of Dade County.

Due to FEMA's inability to deal with the disaster, the military was asked to step in and take a leading role. Ultimately, over 23,000 troops provided assistance in Florida's recovery efforts. The navy sent bulldozers, backhoes (powerful vehicles that can scoop up large amounts of dirt and debris), and flatbeds to remove debris. The Coast Guard responded to over 70 distress calls during and after the hurricane, including one that led to the rescue of four Cubans from a raft being tossed about in rough seas.

The army sent 100,000 meals-ready-to-eat (MREs) almost immediately after Andrew's arrival, but they did not get to the food distribution centers because state and local agencies were not ready to provide transportation from the airports. By the end of the week, 5,000 troops had flown in from Fort Bragg, North Carolina, with medical supplies, helicopters, bulldozers, and 20 portable kitchens that could prepare three meals a day for 6,000 people. Military specialists in medicine, engineering, and aviation, along with those who would supervise the provision of food and lodging in tent cities, were among those sent to Florida.

Once runways were cleared at Homestead Air Force Base, cargo planes landed every 20 minutes or so, bringing in another 7,000 army and marine troops with tents, a combat hospital, and more field kitchens. These troops assisted with traffic flow, provided meals, and treated the sick and injured. The military shipped in enough tents to provide shelter for 10,000 people in two tent cities. An additional 6,500

National Guard troops were mobilized to help overworked law enforcement officers maintain order.

The Army Corps of Engineers played a critical role in the recovery and reconstruction efforts after the hurricane. The corps provided 55 million square feet (5.1 million m²) of roofing material that was used to secure 22,000 homes from the rain. Over 2,000 trucks per day hauled away debris—a total of 12 million cubic yards (9.2 million m³). In addition, the corps provided 250 travel trailers for temporary housing, 5,400 portable toilets, hundreds of shower facilities, and washers and dryers to clean clothing. In cooperation with military service personnel and many volunteers, the corps repaired 268 of 278 Dade County schools, enabling them to open for classes just three weeks after Andrew struck. The recovery efforts of the corps cost $400 million in federal funds.

Nongovernmental Response

Over two dozen nonprofit and charitable organizations swung into action in the days just before Andrew struck. Along with government agencies, these organizations provided residents with shelter, food, water, and medical care.

The Red Cross opened over 30 shelters before Andrew's arrival. However, Red Cross volunteers were unable to assist because they had hurricane problems of their own. As a result, shelters were crowded and understaffed. Despite initial staffing problems, within the first week of the recovery effort Red Cross volunteers provided 280,000 meals. By the time that the relief effort wrapped up, 12,175 Red Cross volunteers and staff from all 50 states, Canada, Columbia, and Mexico had worked around the clock, providing 4 million meals. In addition, Red Cross personnel staffed 20 centers that provided 60,149 persons with $46.7 million in assistance. In all, the Red Cross contributed $81.5 million to displaced residents in southern Florida and southern Louisiana.

A Red Cross shelter set up in the Homestead, Florida, middle school became home to hundreds of people in the days and weeks after Hurricane Andrew flattened all but a few of the buildings in town. (Photo courtesy of Associated Press)

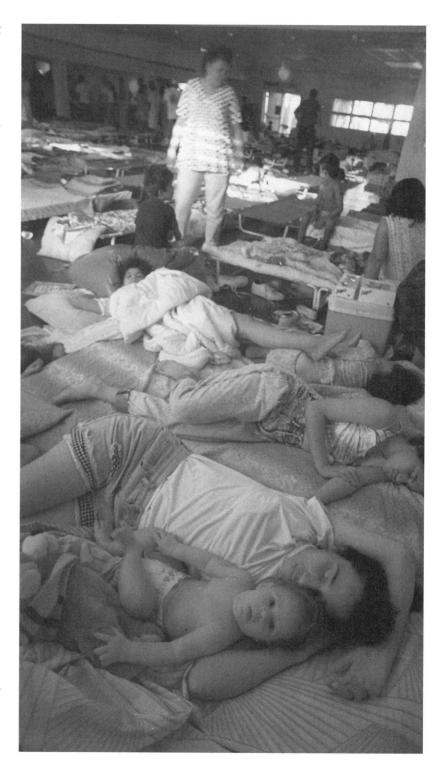

A number of other relief organizations also provided significant assistance. The Salvation Army's Operation Reconstruction provided 120 million pounds (54.4 million kg) of relief supplies (even though the Salvation Army itself had to flee from Andrew—its Fort Lauderdale shelter was in the flood zone). In the Cutler Ridge area, the Salvation Army provided two 5,000-gallon (18,900-l) water trucks that spent each day distributing clean water to residents.

The Second Harvest Food Bank of Orlando, Florida, provided 56,000 meals within the first week. The United Way provided 70,000 volunteers. Twenty-six different organizations—including the home-building Habitat for Humanity—joined together to form the Reconstruction Alliance. By pooling their resources, these organizations were able to coordinate their assistance to the neediest families. The "Best Possible Donation" sidebar below tells of the best donations to make following a disaster.

The Best Possible Donation

Seeing the destruction wrought by Hurricane Andrew on television, people from around the nation were moved to help. Donations from around the country flooded in to Florida and southern Louisiana. Unfortunately, many people sent clothing, thinking that they were helping the needy. Tons of clothing arrived, but there was no safe place to store it or any way to distribute it. With so many buildings leaking, poorly stored clothing got wet and started to mildew. In the end, piles of clothing were bulldozed together and burned to get them out of the way. Louisiana started turning down clothing donations within a few days.

During emergencies, charities can always use money to purchase what is needed—and it does not take up valuable storage space. Therefore, it is always best to make a cash donation when contributing to disaster relief.

CHAPTER 4

Lives Disrupted

Palm Beach Police Department search-and-rescue expert Ed Rigolo and his dog, Mara, sift through a wreckage site on August 26, 2002, looking for bodies buried underneath the debris. (Photo courtesy of Associated Press)

Although the city of Miami started to return to life just a few hours after Andrew passed through, people in other southern Florida cities, including Homestead, Florida City, and Kendall, were not so lucky. Those who had lived through Andrew's direct hit found their lives blown away: their homes, their businesses, their employment, and the very landmarks that they had taken for granted were all gone. As they returned to the areas where their homes once stood, residents were at a loss to find even a scrap of anything familiar. The hardest-hit residents found themselves with nothing: no food, no water, no shelter. Many possessed only the clothes that they were wearing when they escaped. In the immediate aftermath of the storm, life meant trying to survive.

Homes Destroyed

Andrew destroyed or seriously damaged over 130,000 residences in the area south of Miami: 85,000 houses, 38,000 apartments, and 11,000 mobile homes. In Homestead, blocks of buildings and five mobile home parks were completely swept away—only the foundations and piles of rubble remained. In one West Kendall neighborhood of 1,000 homes, only a few survived without damage. Most simply disintegrated. Just south of the Tamiami Airport, 50 acres (20.2 ha) of land holding trailer parks were left with piles of sheet-metal siding—most completely unidentifiable as trailers.

Rescuers desperately needed to reach these areas to look for people who had decided to ride out the storm in their homes and might be hurt or trapped in rubble. They needed to get to these hard-hit areas quickly, but it was unsafe to drive on debris-filled roads. Within days after Andrew hit, rescue teams had been able to search through only 15 percent of the devastated area. They brought in dogs trained to sniff out any missing people—dead or alive. Although there were hundreds of rumors of people trapped in debris, in fact, most people had evacuated the area. Rescuers found only a few people who had died during the storm. The fate of pets during the hurricane is told in the "What about the Pets?" sidebar on page 36.

One man was lucky. To escape the hurricane, he had driven his car into a concrete warehouse where he thought that he would be safe. When the concrete roof collapsed, he was trapped in his car. Once Andrew had passed through, he started to listen for any sign of people. The first people on the scene were looters—people taking advantage of the damage to steal whatever they could. The looters heard the man's screams for help and alerted police officers in the area. Once rescue workers arrived on the scene, it took them 30 minutes to free him.

Since almost all the residents survived the storm, even though their homes did not, the first problem was finding adequate shelter.

What about the Pets?

People were not the only ones who were lost in an alien landscape. When residents evacuated and left for shelters, their pets had to be left behind—shelters did not take pets. While some horseracing tracks in the area were able to take in horses for boarding in their sturdy barns, dogs and cats were not so lucky. Those that survived the storm wandered around, looking for their families and trying to find food to eat. Unfortunately, with the turmoil surrounding the relocation of thousands of homeless people, many pets could not be reunited with their owners. Those that remained unclaimed were rounded up and destroyed.

In the first few days after Andrew passed through, over 250,000 people were homeless—or 10 percent of the population of Dade County. Within a week at least 150,000 were still homeless. The other 100,000 had sought temporary shelter with friends and family who lived outside the destruction zone.

Tens of thousands of people decided to stay in their damaged homes, despite the lack of roofs, windows, and doors to keep the rain and wind out. They were afraid that if they left what little they had, looters would take their possessions. Many people also did not want to live in tent cities, where they would have little privacy. Therefore, residents secured what was left of their homes with sheets of plastic and plywood, while walls and ceilings of wet plaster collapsed around them. They had no electricity, no running water, and no sanitation facilities.

The army started raising tent cities on August 30—complete with adequate sanitation, kitchens, and showers. The tent cities were to help those who needed it most—people with no shelter. There were enough cots and tents to house 20,000 people. An additional 2,000 people were still living at Red Cross shelters. As it became apparent that they would not be able to leave within a few days, shelter residents began to refer to hallways and corners of shelters as "home."

Those most desperate for housing—the very poor who had been residents of migrant worker camps—had no opportunities for emergency shelter. They had no transportation, lived miles away from the shelters, and did not understand English well enough to get basic information. Because of their rural locations, emergency workers did not reach these people as quickly as those in larger cities.

Another major problem was debris—tons of it—that had been blown by Andrew's powerful winds and caused major damage. Flying material from buildings that had been blown apart had ruined many of the buildings that were left standing. The navy responded with bulldozers, backhoes, and flatbed trucks to haul away the worst of the debris. However, debris removal was of secondary importance when compared with providing clean water, fresh food, and medical assistance to homeless families. Since the debris included rotting food from people's homes, rats came in large numbers to scavenge among the wreckage for something to eat. Standing water attracted mosquitoes. The problems facing Andrew's survivors were just beginning.

Necessities of Life

Southern Dade County had become a land with no place to buy food, water, or gasoline. Although water, food, and medicines were flooding into the area, problems organizing their distribution prevented those needing these items from getting them.

Clean water was in critically short supply. Dade County residents who finally had running water a week after the storm still had to boil it to make it safe. In the rest of the county, the lack of electricity meant that there was no way to pump water from wells. People stood in line for hours just to get a couple of liters of water to drink.

Food and the ice to keep it safe were also hard to find, due to distribution problems. Just three days after Andrew hit, a despairing Governor Chiles noted that the state had received an emergency shipment of 120,000 C-rations (packaged meals that do not need refrigeration), but no one within the state government knew where they had been stored. People often spent several hours a day looking for food and ice. Often, they stood in line at relief centers or at army field kitchens that were serving food.

Some people, desperate for something to eat, just took what they could find from damaged stores. Again, poor residents were the ones least able to reach food sources due to lack of transportation. With both offices of the Department of Health and Rehabilitative Services destroyed, the poor were not able to get the food stamps needed to purchase food, if they could find a store with some to sell.

The third immediate critical problem besides food and water was health care. Almost all the hospitals in the area had been damaged and were without power to provide essential services to

U.S. Marines erected a tent camp in Homestead, Florida, which thousands of Hurricane Andrew survivors called home until their own homes could be rebuilt. (Photo courtesy of Associated Press)

patients. Defense Department officials stepped in with generators to restore electricity to the affected hospitals, but many medical employees were unable to reach their workplaces. Medical personnel who had been on duty during the hurricane's passage were still on duty 36 hours later, providing emergency medical care to the wounded.

Flying glass and other debris had caused many of the cuts and bruises being seen in hospital emergency rooms and clinics. However, most of the injuries occurred during the cleanup and recovery phase. People fell off roofs that they were repairing, cut themselves with chainsaws while sawing up fallen trees, or were hurt by falling ceilings while living in their damaged homes. Children in migrant labor camps were suffering from prickly heat (a condition caused by overheating that leads to extremely itchy, stinging skin) or getting sick due to poor sanitation and scarcity of clean water. These problems were made worse by the lack of medical facilities in very poor neighborhoods.

Gnats, flies, mosquitoes, rats, and other vermin became a greater problem over time, as standing water, rotting food and dead animals, and human waste remained untreated. Public health officials sprayed for mosquitoes to prevent possible outbreaks of the diseases encephalitis and malaria—both spread by infected mosquitoes. Keeping mosquitoes out of homes was a major problem. Without windows and doors on living spaces, mosquitoes were easily able to find their targets—people—for quick meals.

With hospitals closed, medical teams set up clinics to deal with the injured. The military brought in two field hospitals and three medical helicopters to evacuate the seriously injured to hospitals outside the worst-hit areas. Doctors and nurses were so overwhelmed with treating immediate problems that they had no time to discuss with people how to prevent the heat stroke and diarrhea that were appearing, due to lack of air-conditioning and poor sanitation.

The problem of handling sewage increased as the amount of food and water increased. Running water was not available, area sewage systems were not working, and there were too few portable toilets for the tens of thousands of homeless people. As a result, human waste was everywhere, creating unhealthy conditions. The navy shipped in 4,600 more portable toilets to add to those already supplied by the Army Corps of Engineers in order to help meet the need. Public health personnel were concerned that poor sanitation could trigger epidemics of diphtheria and hepatitis—diseases spread by contaminated water and food. The situation was most dangerous to children with poor immune systems. Medical teams reported that large numbers of children were suffering from diarrhea, dehydration, and ear and upper respiratory infections. With pharmacies closed, medicines were difficult to find. Effects to people's mental health are related in the "Andrew's Mental Health Effects" sidebar below.

Andrew's Mental Health Effects

Not only did injuries and physical illnesses need treatment after the hurricane, but there was also an increase in mental health problems due to stress, anxiety, and depression as people struggled to cope with daily life. Children who had been extremely frightened by the high winds and noise of the storm suffered from post-traumatic stress disorder (PTSD)—a mental illness that sometimes results when people have endured a life-threatening event. There were not enough mental health professionals to care for all those who needed help. Widespread symptoms of mental illness persisted for two months after Andrew's appearance. A year later, 33 percent of Dade County children were still clinically depressed. Stressed adults also had problems: the divorce rate increased by 15 percent and domestic violence incidents rose 21 percent in the months following the hurricane. Once the physical cuts and bruises were healed, the emotional hurts lingered. Patricia Regester, director of the Mental Health Association of Dade County, told Psychology Today: "What people don't understand is we've got years and years of rebuilding people. We've got to deal with people damage."

Utilities and Roads Wiped Away

Power, water, sanitation, transportation, and medical care facilities in southern Dade County were almost entirely destroyed by Andrew. Indeed, the southern part of Dade County was completely cut off from civilization. Restoring basic services to residents took months, not weeks. Southern Louisiana also suffered some damage to utilities, but basic electrical and water services were back online within a few days of the hurricane.

Andrew destroyed 3,300 miles (5,310 km) of power lines in Dade County. The cities of Homestead and Florida City, just 20 miles (32.2 km) south of Miami, had no electricity at all. With the help of an additional 2,000 utility workers from northern Florida and other states, Florida Power and Light (FP&L) worked around the clock to restore power. However, a week after the hurricane, 275,000 people were still without power. FP&L repaired the most accessible lines first, but crews were frustrated that they could not even reach many areas to determine the extent of the damage.

The power problems were greater than just downed power poles and broken power lines. Two large electrical generating plants were severely damaged; repairs took more than six months. FP&L had to replace in just a few months an electrical grid that had taken 50 years to build. Reinforced concrete power poles had been snapped off at their bases. The company needed 6.6 million feet (2 million m) of power line just to route electricity throughout the county—and another 2.2 million feet (670,000 m) of line to connect houses to new power poles. Ten thousand new transformers, 18,000 new wooden utility poles, and 180,000 ceramic sleeves to insulate the wires from the poles were also needed.

The water supply system was also badly affected by the storm. Although the pipes were underground, over 3,300 water mains were damaged and required repair. Some areas had no running water, and in places where water did flow through the pipes, it was contaminated.

Equally serious problems affected transportation routes and communication services. With streets impassable due to wrecked cars, downed trees, and flooding, it took all day to drive the 40 miles (64.4 km) from Florida City to Miami and back. Traffic signals—at least the ones that had not blown away—could not work without power. Transportation officials estimated that 150,000 street and traffic signs had been destroyed in 42,000 places. The cost to replace them was $50 million. Surface traffic was not the only transportation problem. South Florida's airports were littered with toppled planes, damaged hangars, and ruined radar gear. Miami's elevated train system was also shut down—some of the tracks were dangling from trestles after having been torn apart by the wind.

Telephone service was limited. There were no working telephones at all in the hardest-hit areas. Residents would drive or walk to use the few pay phones that were still working, only to

Downed power lines were just one part of Dade County's electrical problem. Once workers laid new lines and planted new utility poles, two generating plants still took six months to repair. (Photo courtesy of National Oceanic and Atmospheric Administration/Department of Commerce)

discover that once a phone was full of quarters, calls could be made only with a phone card. With over 17,000 phones out of service, Southern Bell brought in 200 more repair people from Georgia and the Carolinas to restore communication lines quickly.

Schools and hospitals also suffered significant damage. Some 10,000 children found themselves with no school to return to once school started in the fall—30 of 237 school buildings in South Florida were severely damaged. Those students had to be bused to other schools, where they attended classes in shifts. A week after Andrew hit, only one hospital out of the seven in southern Dade County was open. The largest hospital in the area, Deering Hospital, was so damaged that it had to be completely closed for repairs. Medical personnel relocated to makeshift clinics in schools and shelters until their offices could be rebuilt.

Counting the Personal Cost

The people who died during Hurricane Andrew were killed by falling and flying debris and by coming into contact with downed electrical wires. At least 30 people died of natural causes—for example, heart attacks—before, during, or immediately after the storm because they were unable to get medical help in time. Most people who die during hurricanes are those who are drowned by storm surge waters, but this was not the case with Andrew. Lives were saved because hundreds of thousands of people evacuated, getting out of the storm's way in time.

However, the suffering continued for thousands of survivors who were left with the shells of damaged houses in which to live. Employers struggled to maintain their businesses without employees. The personal suffering of the people of Dade County would be compounded by the loss of the local economy. Andrew may have passed through in a few hours, but the hurricane's effects would live on for years.

CHAPTER 5

The Economy: Destroyed by Wind and Water

This aerial photograph of Dade County illustrates how Hurricane Andrew literally ripped the roof off every house for miles around. (Photo courtesy of National Oceanic Atmospheric Administration/ Department of Commerce)

After Andrew, the repair and rebuilding of homes, businesses, factories, utilities, and transportation and communications networks would take time and require adequate funds from insurers and loans from the federal government. The economy—the producer of wealth, the provider of employment—would not be so easily replaced. Businesses whose buildings had been seriously damaged no longer had merchandise or services to sell. Their employees were left without work. Factories could not produce

goods without electricity and running water. Marinas, home to thousands of pleasure boats, would need to completely rebuild before once again serving the sailing public. Hotels and resorts were unable to meet the needs of tourists. The areas hit by Andrew left business in ruins.

The Bahamas—A Slightly Damaged Economy

Had Andrew been a large hurricane, it would have caused extensive damage on many of the islands that form the Bahamas. However, because it was a compact hurricane, only two of the islands took a direct hit, and the damage to the Bahamian economy from this storm was relatively light. Tourists did leave abruptly just before the hurricane's arrival, which resulted in loss of revenue from those visitors. However, resort areas did not experience significant damage and were able to welcome visitors in the fall and winter—the busiest time of the tropical tourist season.

On Eleuthera, marinas and the boats tied up there were damaged by the pounding waves and the storm surge. However, damage could have been much worse had Andrew been a larger storm and moved more slowly. Andrew caused no long-term adverse effect on the economy in the Bahamas.

Florida—A True Business Disaster

In Florida, despite the huge amount of damage, Andrew's compactness and quick passage lessened its impact. In other words, economic damage could have been much worse had the hurricane been slower-moving and more massive. The damage could also have been much worse had the eye passed over Miami instead of the relatively underdeveloped areas in southern Dade County. However, Andrew did severely impact an area that was already struggling economically in the early 1990s.

The destruction of Homestead Air Force Base by Hurricane Andrew left hundreds without work, further harming the already struggling economy of Dade County. (Photo courtesy of National Oceanic Atmospheric Administration/ Department of Justice)

In 1992 Homestead Air Force Base was a major contributor to Dade County's economy. Located on 3,600 acres (1,460 ha) of land sandwiched between Miami and Everglades National Park, it directly employed 7,500 people and pumped $406 million annually into the local area. In addition to its active-duty military and civilian employees, the presence of the base encouraged over 20,000 military retirees to remain in the area. The incomes of these people also poured into the region's economy.

Andrew changed all that when it scored a direct hit on the air force base on August 24, 1992. Flyable aircraft had all been flown to safety before Andrew's arrival, so they had not been lost. But aircraft hangars, communications facilities, office and maintenance buildings, housing—almost every building on the base was flattened. As Toni Riordan, a representative of the State

Community Affairs Department, succinctly put it, "Homestead AFB no longer exists." The eventual fate of the base is related in the "Rebuilding Homestead?" sidebar on page 48.

Dade County is a major agricultural center for Florida, growing tropical fruit, row crops (for example, tomatoes), and ornamental plants and houseplants. Andrew ripped through this carefully cultivated land and destroyed tens of millions of dollars of crops and orchards. The wind uprooted groves of trees, which were carried west until they landed with their root systems pointing up into the sky. They looked like giant twigs that had been tossed into a huge jumble.

All of the tropical fruit groves experienced at least some damage; the Persian lime, avocado, and mango groves were hit the worst. Almost 95 percent of all limes grown in the United States come from groves near Homestead, Florida. Before the hurricane, over 6,000 acres (2,430 ha) were planted with lime groves—afterward, only 1,700 acres (690 ha) were left. Most of the trees were stripped of their fruit and leaves. Others were just blown down. "It looked horrible," lamented citrus processor Larry Murray, "like someone had taken a chainsaw to most of the trees." Fortunately, most of Florida's citrus crop was north of Andrew's path, but over $20 million in limes was lost. Although the acreage in limes had increased to almost 2,700 acres (1,090 ha) by the late 1990s, most of that total acreage has since been destroyed by a tree-killing disease unrelated to Andrew, known as lime canker.

Andrew also ruined one-third of the avocado acreage, which still has not recovered to pre-Andrew levels, even though avocados make up half of all tropical fruit acreage in Dade County. The introduction of imported avocados from Mexico and the opportunity to sell acreage at a profit for building suburban communities have encouraged some farmers not to replant lost avocado orchards. Other orchards were allowed to return to woodland, with no active cultivation taking place, because the orchard owners decided that it was not profitable to clear the debris and replant the trees.

Rebuilding Homestead?

Within a few days of the hurricane, President George H.W. Bush announced that Homestead Air Force Base would be rebuilt. That news cheered local residents, but before long, the military announced that it would not rebuild Homestead. Unfortunately for the base, the early 1990s were a period of military *downsizing* (the number of military bases was being reduced). The Pentagon had no interest in spending millions of dollars to rebuild a base when it was closing down other bases in the country. With the exception of a few jobs that remained to staff the reserve unit that settled there, most of the base's 7,500 employees and their families were transferred to new assignments. As Homestead city manager Curt Ivy put it, "The reserve base is very good, but it's not the size of what we had before." He would like to see the rest of the base used for housing developments, a mall, office space, or perhaps a film studio.

The hurricane destroyed one-third of the mango acreage, as well, reducing the harvest from 11 tons (10 mt) of fruit worth $4.3 million before the hurricane to 1.4 tons (1.25 mt) worth less than $1 million a year after it passed through. Andrew blew off the fruit and leaves, broke major branches, and split tree trunks. Some trees were toppled completely, and those that stood suffered severe bark scars from blowing debris. The remaining weakened trees, exposed to the heat of the Sun, suffered heat stress and sunburn that contributed to the overall decline of the orchards. Mango orchards were slow to recover, because trees continued to die for several years after the initial hurricane damage occurred.

Tropical fruit orchards were not the only agricultural sector to see significant damage. The houseplant industry, a $150-million-a-year operation before Andrew, took large losses. Not only were the plants ruined, but so were the buildings in which they were cultivated. This industry has since been successfully reconstructed as new greenhouses have been built and plant production has been increased. Row crops, including many of the vegetables sold in South Florida's grocery stores, were also wiped out, and competition from Mexican growers under the North American Free Trade Agreement (NAFTA), combined with land development pressures, has adversely affected this sector's ability to return to pre-Andrew levels of production.

In addition to losses sustained by the air force base and agriculture, Andrew damaged or destroyed over 82,000 businesses in southern Florida. With Biscayne and Everglades National Parks closed for months after the hurricane, the tourist industry withered. Shopping centers in Cutler Ridge and Homestead were knocked down during the storm, and looters took the merchandise that remained. The Homestead Sports Complex, home to some of the Olympic trials in baseball, was badly damaged. Fruit-packing houses—dependent upon farming for their business—were severely hurt. Among the businesses that were able to survive with advanced planning were computing centers. By temporarily transferring their duties to other centers, they were able to deal with the power and communications outages until they were fixed.

Many of southern Florida's business problems after Andrew were made worse by the state of business before Andrew. Many businesses were already suffering financially and thus were not in position to secure new loans when their buildings and inventories were damaged during the hurricane.

Louisiana—The Flow Is Slowed

Andrew came ashore in Louisiana as a category 3 hurricane, so its winds were not as powerful as they had been in Florida. However, they were strong enough to do considerable damage to sugarcane fields, oil-drilling rigs in the Gulf of Mexico, and offshore fisheries. The damage to the fisheries is described in the "A Fishy Loss" sidebar on page 51.

Southern Louisiana's sugarcane crop was almost ready for harvest when Andrew arrived. Almost 400,000 acres (161,900 ha) of sugarcane with a market value of $90 million were flattened. The actual loss—considering the lost harvest and cleaning up the mess that was left behind—reached almost $200 million, or almost 20 percent of Louisiana's damage from the hurricane.

Hurricane Andrew dumped up to 10 inches (25 cm) of rain in some parts of Louisiana, causing flooding in St. Mary Parish. (Photo courtesy of Associated Press)

Although offshore, not in Louisiana proper, petroleum industry losses were directly tied to the state. Anticipating the arrival of Andrew, workers on the 3,700 drilling rigs and platforms in the Gulf of Mexico turned off all the equipment, stopped production, and evacuated. Andrew's winds and high seas battered the drilling rigs, separating platforms from their footings (where they connect to the seafloor). In all, 120 petroleum platforms were damaged. For two to three days, there was no production at all.

The gulf petroleum fields produce about 23 percent of the nation's daily output of natural gas—almost 12 billion cubic feet (340 million m³). Much of the natural gas pumped out of the gulf is piped directly to refineries in Louisiana. When drilling stopped in the gulf, gas stopped flowing to the refineries. Initially, industry executives thought that production would be reduced by about 1 billion cubic feet (28.3 million m³) per day, but this estimate was quickly revised upward to 2.5 billion–2.75 billion cubic feet (70.1–77.8 million m³) per day for at least two weeks. This drop in production reduced the nation's natural gas output by about 5 percent per day.

The storm also reduced crude oil production in the region by one-third. In addition to the damaged petroleum rigs, a major pipeline ruptured in the coastal waters just 30 miles (48.3 km) south of Louisiana. Any of the rigs that had pumped their petroleum through the line had to wait to resume production until it was fixed. Not including the lost production, the petroleum industry losses were estimated to be $100 million. Losses would have been greater had the federal government not passed stringent construction standards in 1976, which allowed the petroleum rigs to withstand much higher winds and waves than had been possible in the past.

A Fishy Loss

Louisiana also lost $100 million in fisheries. As Andrew swept past, it stirred up sediment at the bottom of both coastal and inland waters, depriving the fish living there of the oxygen that they needed to survive. Tens of thousands of fish died. Dead saltwater fish lined the coastline for miles, and acres of dead and dying freshwater fish floated on the surface of the Atchafalaya Basin, Bayou Lafourche, and Lake Verrett. Oyster reefs and the oyster crop experienced significant damage from turbulent waters and sediments that were deposited over these shellfish.

CHAPTER 6

Unique Ecosystems Washed Away

Complex and fragile ecosystems in Biscayne National Park suffered great damage from Hurricane Andrew when oil and motor fuel leaked from boats that had been tossed about in the storm. (Photo courtesy of Associated Press)

In just two hours, Hurricane Andrew roared through three national parks on the southern Florida peninsula—parks that represented diverse ecosystems of national importance. They encompass barrier reefs; coral reefs and sea grass beds; shallow lagoons; mangrove forests; pine, hardwood, and cypress forests; and seasonal freshwater marshes. Each ecosystem responded differently to the raging winds and storm surge of Andrew. Those that were already stressed by human actions, such as the Everglades, were

more severely damaged by Andrew. Some, like the marine environments of eastern Florida, suffered less damage than usual during a hurricane, because Andrew moved through quickly and caused less disturbance of the water. This reduced the movement of sand along the bottom and reduced the number of fish deaths.

Florida's National Parks

Biscayne National Park, Everglades National Park, and Big Cypress National Preserve all suffered significant ecological and aesthetic damage as a result of Andrew. As an offshore park, Biscayne's water quality suffered as oil and motor fuel leaked from boats that had been tossed around on the rough seas. The churning waters stirred up sediment and decaying organic materials, robbing the water of oxygen and forcing fish to the surface and lobsters to the shore. Surprisingly, sea grasses, algae, and corals living in 6.6 feet (2 m) of water remained healthy, while plants on the shore just 32.8 feet (10 m) away were destroyed. Thrown about by the surf, resident fish were scraped and bruised, but very few died. The fast-moving Andrew did not have time to produce the violent wave action associated with most hurricanes—thus, plants and animals immediately offshore soon returned to their normal life patterns.

Although low-growing trees and shrubs on the land weathered the storm, many taller mangrove trees—in the range of 32.8–49.2 feet (10–15 m)—were destroyed. Biscayne and Everglades National Parks together lost a total of 70,000 acres (28,330 ha) of mangroves, which were either completely knocked over or severely damaged. The most significant damage occurred near Andrew's center, where the wind was strongest—80 to 95 percent of the trees near the center were destroyed when the trunks snapped or were uprooted.

Trees and fish both fared poorly in Everglades National Park, although saw grass growing in the interior freshwater *wetlands* and most terrestrial animals came through without too many problems. In addition to the downed mangroves, one-fourth of the royal palms and one-third of the pine trees were broken or damaged by the wind. This created space for other species of trees to grow, as told in the "Alien Species Borne on the Wind" sidebar below. Interior wetlands, adversely affected in previous hurricanes, experienced little damage because the storm surge of saltwater did not reach deep into the park.

Because the 50 endangered Florida panthers living in the park wore radio transmitters on special collars, park officials were able

Alien Species Borne on the Wind

Starting in the 1920s, Florida governor Napoleon Bonaparte Broward encouraged Floridians to import tropical trees as part of his campaign to drain the Everglades and create more land for development. These trees grew faster than the native mangroves. They have now taken over 100,000 acres (40,500 ha) of land bordering the northern part of the Everglades. Naturalists now realize that these *alien plants* can crowd out the native mangroves and alter the natural conditions of the Everglades.

During Hurricane Andrew, seeds from eucalyptus, Brazilian pepper plants, and Australian pines blew deep into the Everglades. Because the many downed trees created new spaces, the seeds had places to sprout and take root. Park officials had to look for these seedlings and pull them out before they took over and choked out the native plants. Because they can survive in less water than the native mangroves, and water levels fall in the Everglades as the population increases, these alien species could dominate the landscape and change the habitat. For example, Australian pines tend to thrive in places that are important turtle nesting areas and force the turtles to lay their eggs elsewhere. This could reduce the turtle population in the future.

to locate all of them and determine that they were safe. Likewise, the park's large deer population emerged unscathed. There was little damage to crocodile nesting sites, sea turtle nesting sites were disturbed but not adversely affected, and no manatees were lost. Although gauging the effect on bird life was difficult, most birds apparently took cover in low-growing shrubs to ride out the storm. Tree loss was considered a potential problem for the nesting of the endangered red-cockaded woodpecker and the black-whiskered vireo, but other species were thought to be in good shape.

Construction and agriculture in southern Florida had been causing stress in the Everglades for years as water was diverted away from the interior swamps and marshes. Scientists were concerned that post-hurricane reconstruction could worsen the water flow conditions in the Everglades, compounding the hurricane damage. David Simon, the natural resources program director of the National Parks and Conservation Association, acknowledged that hurricanes had been part of the Everglades' environment for thousands of years, but that "the question after this storm will be whether Andrew has delivered a knockout blow to an ecosystem that's dangerously stressed already."

Big Cypress National Preserve suffered less damage than the other two parks because most of its stands of pine trees were north of Andrew's center. However, the southern part of the preserve, known as Lostmans Pines, was heavily damaged. In that area, Andrew blew over 40 percent of all trees with diameters greater than 9.8 inches (25 cm).

Effects on Florida's Ecosystems

Andrew's winds blew hard and the surf was rough, but the hurricane's forward movement was so fast that it did not move extensive amounts of sediment on the coastal seafloor or along the shoreline. Although such sand movement is a normal process along the coast, too much movement too fast can create problems for both people

The Everglades forest in South Florida was already an ecosystem under stress before Hurricane Andrew thundered through the area. Scientists and environmentalists are watching the area carefully to see if there will be any long-term damage from the storm. (Photo courtesy of Associated Press)

and wildlife. Earlier, weaker hurricanes had lingered over the coastline and caused considerable damage due to shifting sand, but luckily Andrew did not cause a great deal of erosion.

However, the surging water did cause significant damage to artificial reefs that had been placed in offshore waters to attract fish. One artificial reef, the Kavorkian Wreck—a 75-foot (23-m) fishing vessel that had been sunk in 69 feet (21 m) of water just outside the Biscayne National Park boundary in 1974—was totally broken apart. Its pieces were pushed 230 feet (70 m) toward the park and into a natural coral reef. Natural reefs fared better than their artificial cousins. Even though some coral reefs detached from the seabed, were overturned, or broke apart, most of the reefs experienced little damage and continued to provide homes for aquatic life.

Reduced water quality in near-shore areas, some areas of intense *scouring* (movement of bottom material by rough water), and beach *overwash* (storm surge waters penetrating past the normal high-tide mark) adversely affected marine resources. Rotting mangrove debris filled the water, which remained extremely murky for a month after Andrew's passing. The debris robbed the water of oxygen and made it difficult for fish and vertebrates to breathe.

For the most part, Andrew did not harm land animals. Baby alligators that had hatched in the week or two before Andrew died in large numbers, however. Washed away from their mothers, they were not capable of surviving on their own. Large wading birds, including herons, wood storks, and roseate spoonbills, were not seen in the weeks following the storm. The lack of bird life concerned wildlife biologists, but the lack of bodies led them to conclude that most of the birds had either flown off before the storm or hidden in the brush while it passed through. The hurricane did damage rookeries (nesting areas), but the basic habitat survived, and the birds rebuilt their nests.

Andrew inflicted greater damage on terrestrial plants. Within the path of the hurricane's center, almost all the large hardwood trees that had been located on *hammocks* (islands of dense tropical undergrowth) were completely *defoliated* (stripped of their leaves). A quarter of them were either pulled up and thrown by the wind or badly broken. The taller the tree, the more damaged it was likely to be. Despite the defoliation, most of the surviving trees and shrubs started to show signs of new growth within three weeks.

Ecosystem Damage in Louisiana

Louisiana is an ecologically sensitive area. Over 40 percent of all coastal wetlands in the United States are located in southern Louisiana. As Andrew passed over the coastline, its winds, tides, and wave action damaged large areas of coastal marshes. Some of

Alien seeds blown into the Everglades by Hurricane Andrew's strong winds could grow into trees that affect the already low water levels in the forest. The lives of many plants and animals like this baby alligator will be threatened if the water dips any lower. (Photo courtesy of Associated Press)

the damage occurred when saltwater poured into low-lying freshwater areas, killing or seriously harming plants.

As the hurricane moved over the Atchafalaya River Basin, home to the largest hardwood swamp—1.5 million acres (607,000 ha)—in the United States, it severely damaged willows and cypress trees living near the coastline. Over 80 percent of the coastal canopy trees were knocked down, compared to just 30 percent that were knocked down only 20 miles (32.2 km) inland. The canopy trees protected the smaller understory trees and saplings that grew beneath, so these came through the storm undamaged. The taller canopy trees were home to young squirrels, which suffered a large death toll. Wildlife biologists estimate that between 50 and 75 percent of all the young squirrels that were born earlier in the summer died during Andrew. However, other mammals did not suffer a significantly high death rate.

Unlike fish in Florida, both fresh- and saltwater fish in Louisiana sustained large losses. Approximately 182 million freshwater fish suffocated in the first 24 hours after Andrew stirred up sediment that deprived the fish of oxygen. Fish continued to die over the next two weeks as the oxygen-deprived water moved into other areas. The dead fish were valued at $160 million. An additional 9.4 million saltwater fish worth almost $8 million died, probably from suffocation when the sediment pulled up by the storm clogged their gills. Their bodies littered a 5-mile (8-km) stretch of coastline just southeast of Andrew's landfall.

The hurricane caused significant beach erosion and sand movement on barrier islands off the Louisiana coast. Andrew washed away 30 percent of the Isles Dernieres. The western islands, which were closer to the hurricane's storm track, experienced greater changes in shape and size than did the eastern islands. One of the eastern islands was completely submerged by the storm surge, and the shoreline moved 223 feet (68 m) inland as the sand washed away.

The overwashing of the islands by the storm surge picked up sand from the fronts of the islands and deposited it on their opposite sides. The resulting movement of sand changed the preexisting environmental conditions. Some grass communities were completely stripped away and buried. Other grass species were moved to different parts of the islands. Most grasses recovered quickly in their new homes. Grasses on barrier islands play an important role in holding the sand in place. Within a short time, they were already acting to stabilize the new sand surfaces formed by the erosive power of the hurricane. Sand movement also killed large numbers of ghost shrimp, small crustaceans that are an important food source for the wading birds living on the islands. This presented a short-term problem for the birds until the shrimp repopulated the area.

CHAPTER 7

Andrew's Legacy

This aerial photograph, taken on August 24, 1992, illustrates how complete the damage was from Hurricane Andrew. Buildings are crushed, trees left standing are stripped of leaves, and utility poles and lines have all but disappeared. (Photo courtesy of Associated Press)

Recovery teams removed the rubble. Contractors installed trailer-filled villages for the homeless. Electricity once again flowed through the power grid and fresh water gushed out of pipes. Streets teemed with traffic, and boats filled harbors and marinas. Businesses reopened and migrant farm workers returned to the fields. However, life after Andrew would never be quite the same again for those who had lived in its path—particularly the residents of southern Florida.

The Human Side

With the devastation in southern Dade County so complete, many of Andrew's survivors decided that they would be better off moving somewhere else. Over 100,000 people left southern Dade County permanently in the months after Andrew's appearance, including 40 percent of the 27,000 residents of the city of Homestead. Those who had received money from their insurance companies for their lost homes and belongings packed up what they had left and moved north to Broward County. In fact, a total of 230,000 people moved from Dade to Broward. Due to the newly crowded conditions, 100,000 residents of Broward moved farther north to Palm Beach County in the nine years after Andrew. This was a 33 percent increase in migration compared with the nine years prior to Andrew. Palm Beach County's population climbed 31 percent between 1990 and 2000, with most of the newcomers coming from Broward and Dade counties.

As a result of this significant movement of people between counties, the *demographics* (the distribution of ethnic groups and educational backgrounds) also changed. The families most likely to leave southern Dade County were middle-class families because they owned their own homes and those homes had been insured. They had the educational backgrounds that allowed them to move to new areas and find employment. Dade County lost almost $500 million in annual personal income in the year after Andrew. Homestead lost 7,500 middle-class jobs when the air force base closed, and the surrounding area lost another 20,000 middle-class retirees for the same reason.

Those left behind were poor, and the poverty rate climbed rapidly. In the years just after Andrew, 28 percent of the residents of Homestead had less than a ninth-grade education. Therefore, their employment opportunities were limited to minimum-wage jobs—if they could find them at all. Although the population of southern Dade County has now rebounded to be greater than it was before Andrew, the people who moved in had incomes that were 20 to 30 percent lower than the incomes of the people who moved north to Broward or Palm Beach counties.

There were ethnic, as well as economic, changes. In the 10 years after Andrew, the number of Latinos in Broward County increased by 150 percent, and they now make up 20 percent of the population. As they moved in, whites moved north. The percentage of black residents also increased by 72 percent between 1990 and 2000. As a result, Broward became much more ethnically diverse, and did so more quickly than it probably would have if Andrew had not struck southern Dade County.

Many survivors of Hurricane Andrew lost everything but their sense of humor, as this aerial picture illustrates. (Photo courtesy of National Oceanic and Atmospheric Administration/Department of Commerce)

The Business Side

Business was slow to rebuild in southern Dade County, primarily because the area was already in an economic slump before Andrew struck. Dependent upon the air force base, agriculture, and tourism—all of which were wiped out by the hurricane—and with 82,000 businesses destroyed or damaged, Dade's economy struggled to recover.

There were local proposals to turn Homestead Air Force Base into a civilian airport. However, those plans were abandoned because federal funding was not available. No alternative plans have been forthcoming. Part of the base now supports a reserve unit that contributes $100 million to the local economy each year—but that is less than one-fourth the amount that the base contributed before Andrew. Large sections of the base still lie in ruins, and it remains a blighted area in the middle of the rest of the recovery.

The agriculture industry continues to have problems. Farmers are under some pressure to sell off their agricultural land at a significant profit for residential and business development. The loss of these agricultural lands could seriously affect the ability of southern Dade County to provide winter vegetables for the eastern United States. Although produce yields are generally up, the amount of planted land is less than it was before Andrew. Ornamental nurseries have become a bright spot in agriculture. These businesses have been flourishing, meeting the increased demand for landscaping plants.

Biscayne and Everglades National Parks were closed for several months after Andrew, not only because of damage to their natural areas, but because almost all the buildings that hosted visitors and housed park personnel were destroyed. Since the parks were a major tourist draw, and since the transportation system and utilities of Dade County were in such disarray, tourism dropped off dramatically. As of 2004, the industry had not yet recovered. Recreational vehicle (RV) parks were largely wiped out by the storm, and tourists have no place to park their vehicles or camp for the night. To make matters worse, four hurricanes struck Florida during the 2004 season. Two of them, Frances and Jeanne, tracked over southeastern Florida, further hampering tourism with flooding rains.

Therefore, Dade County has looked to different opportunities to improve its economic base. A new addition since Andrew has been the Homestead Motorsports Complex, which features National Association for Stock Car Auto Racing (NASCAR) and Indianapolis-style races. The complex, which has been quite successful, has become a source of cash for the county via the tourists who come to watch the races. The Homestead Sports Complex

In nearby Broward County, population growth stemming from an influx of people displaced by Hurricane Andrew has led to an increase in home construction. (Photo courtesy of Associated Press)

was built before Andrew but suffered significant damage that needed to be repaired. The complex had been the spring training site for Major League Baseball's Cleveland Indians, but the team pulled out after the storm. The complex's managers now rent it out on a short-term basis while they look for a more permanent tenant.

The county has also been actively encouraging small manufacturers like boat builders and high-end tile makers to relocate there. Rents are lower in Dade County than in other parts of Florida, giving business owners an incentive to move south. An additional draw for many employers is the presence of the new permanent campus of the Miami-Dade Community College in Homestead.

The building of new homes remained fairly constant through the fiscal year of 2000–2001, bringing in $15.6 million in builder's permits. In fiscal year 2001–2002, however, the value of permits jumped to $51.8 million and has remained that high since. The addition of a new sewer system will allow even more residential development in the future. As housing costs increase in other locations, people will be drawn back to Dade County.

Andrew seriously damaged homes because they had not been well built. The problem was not with the housing codes themselves, which require homes to be built according to certain safety standards. Sufficient rules governing the building of storm-resistant housing had been law since 1986, but they had not been enforced. A lack of inspectors prevented the close supervision of building practices, which led some contractors to use cheaper materials and faster but less sturdy methods of building than the law required. The result was buildings that could not withstand hurricane-force winds.

Additional new rules and provisions for enforcing them became law in March 2002. These new codes especially addressed the building of houses near the coast—the ones most likely to be in danger from future hurricanes. The idea behind the new regulations is to keep people's homes from disintegrating and to keep debris from flying through the windows of neighbors' homes. No one knows if these measures will be effective, since the area has not been hit by a major hurricane since Andrew. However, although the new rules add thousands of dollars in costs to the average house, enforcement has been dramatically improved. The best building codes mean nothing if they are not enforced.

Because of the large numbers of homes and businesses damaged by Andrew, insurance companies suffered very large financial losses. As a result, a number of insurers pulled their businesses out of South Florida. Those companies that remained drastically increased the amount of their premiums (the amount of money that homeowners and businesses pay for their insurance coverage), sometimes charging two or three times as much as they had before Andrew's arrival. At least eleven insurers became insolvent (meaning that they did not have the money to pay off claims), at

Although most of the economy of Dade County has suffered in the aftermath of Hurricane Andrew, home construction is one area of growth. (Photo courtesy of National Oceanic and Atmospheric Administration/Department of Commerce)

least partly due to losses from Andrew, and those who were still solvent no longer wanted to write insurance policies.

Florida would have had an enormous problem if residents were unable to purchase insurance to guard against the loss of their homes. Therefore, the Florida legislature, with the concurrence of Governor Chiles, passed a law that prevented insurance companies from dropping their customers. The state also established the Florida Residential Property and Casualty Joint Underwriting Association (JUA). JUA issued homeowners' insurance at rates higher than those charged by private insurers, but by 1996 there were more than 1 million people covered by JUA policies because they could not get private insurance. Since the state did not want to be in the insurance business, it started providing subsidies (additional funds) to insurers to persuade them to issue more homeowners' policies, thus reducing the number of people holding JUA policies.

In 2002 a smaller JUA joined another agency that provided insurance against wind damage to form Citizens Property Insurance. This agency remains the last hope of homeowners who cannot get private insurance for their dwellings. To prepare for future emergencies like Andrew, the state also established a catastrophe fund that insurers could draw upon during a major disaster. By 2002, the fund totaled $11 billion to help pay claims from a major hurricane, with another $9.6 billion held in reserve in case another hurricane strikes a year later.

The Environment

At least 20 years will pass before the trees blown over and smashed by Andrew are replaced and have grown back to the size that they were before the hurricane struck. With 90 percent of southern Dade's native pines, mangroves, and tropical hardwood hammocks damaged or destroyed and 30 years' worth of debris scattered in wooded areas (meaning that the amount of debris that Andrew

When Hurricane Andrew uprooted and knocked down trees, many areas were left without natural drainage methods, worrying officials that future flooding might be a problem. It will be at least 20 years before many of the replacement trees reach the size of the specimens destroyed by the hurricane. (Photo courtesy of National Oceanic and Atmospheric Administration/Department of Commerce)

created was the same as would normally have accumulated in 30 years), it will take a while for the environment to fully recover.

The invasion of alien species was a major problem in the months and years following Andrew. Seeds from such species blew into the heart of the Everglades on Andrew's winds. Some of these alien plants force out other plants, and they upset the animal habitats. Park workers must continually monitor for their presence and pull these plants out before they take hold.

In general, the ecosystems damaged by Andrew have been slow to recover. The mangrove forests, in particular, have had a difficult time coming back to their previous form. Although many trees did survive the storm, they gradually died due to damage received when debris from other downed trees blew into them. The hurricane had dispersed *propagules* (special mangrove seeds), but most of the seedlings that sprouted from them were deposited in sediments and sulfides that did not support life. Mangroves have, of course, been hit by many hurricanes in the past, but Andrew caused so much damage—and the wood is so slow to rot (which makes it difficult for new plants to take root)—that the mangroves are not as likely to recover fully this time.

One benefit of the compactness of Andrew was that the storm moved through the area so quickly that saltwater did not move into freshwater swamp areas, thus aiding in swamp recovery. Previous hurricane damage was often followed by massive fires started by lightning strikes, which fed on the huge amounts of fuel left by downed trees. That fires did not follow Andrew was the supreme stroke of luck for the national parks and the ecosystems that they support.

The constant pressure from human populations on the health of the parks was a problem before Andrew and contributed to problems after Andrew. Fuel discharged from wrecked boats and marinas continued to foul waters for at least a month after the hurricane. Additionally, crab and lobster traps that fishermen had set out in advance of Andrew broke loose from their anchors and slammed into coral reefs, causing significant damage during the storm surge. As related in the sidebar "A Small Mountain of Debris" on page 72, the debris from populated areas also negatively affected the parks.

Louisiana's barrier islands have also been slow to recover. The vegetation that covers these islands spreads by sending shoots out from adult plants over barren areas instead of by making seeds that can be blown out over the sand. As a result, these plants, so important for stabilizing the sand, spread very slowly. The shoots extend out only a short distance during the growing season, and nutria (large rodents) were busily chomping on the tender little shoots, preventing their forward advance. However, within two years of the storm, the ghost shrimp population had returned to its pre-Andrew levels. Because ghost shrimp burrow in the sand, they also help to trap grass seeds and thus encourage their spread across the spits of sand.

Hurricane specialist James Franklin demonstrates a device called a Global Positioning System dropwindsonde. The instrument, which is dropped from an airplane flying through a hurricane, measures the strength of winds in order to categorize the storm. (Photo courtesy of Associated Press)

Predicting Future Hurricanes

Hurricane prediction has improved dramatically in the last 20 years, and it will continue to improve as companies design better computers and as atmospheric scientists design better computer models to simulate the movements of hurricanes. However, knowing exactly where a hurricane is going to strike will not prevent damage. Such advanced knowledge will allow for timely evacuations out of danger zones if people heed the warnings and leave their homes when they are told to leave.

One potential issue for hurricane forecasters to consider is the warming of Earth's atmosphere, popularly known as global warming. Warmer air in the tropics will lead to warmer ocean water, larger masses of unstable air, and therefore more hurricanes forming during hurricane season each year. The more hurricanes that form, the more likely it is that some of them will strike the coastal areas of the eastern United States and the Gulf Coast.

Preparing for the Future: Will It Be Enough?

Realistically, there is no way to build a building that will survive a direct hit by a category 5 hurricane without any damage. Furthermore, homes built in coastal areas that can be reached by a large storm surge will always be in danger of being destroyed—whether the hurricane makes a direct hit on them or not.

Nonetheless, building standards need to be much tougher in coastal areas, and builders must be held accountable for meeting them. Florida has taken major steps in strengthening building codes and enforcement, but all of the states along the Atlantic coastline need to take similar measures. In addition, states along the gulf coast and the Atlantic seaboard need to decide how many buildings they will allow near the coastline—buildings that will ultimately have to be replaced due to hurricane damage. Once the memories of past hurricane damage fades away, some people may attempt to weaken building codes to reduce the costs of new construction. Indeed, the Florida Building Commission tried to introduce a new statewide building code in 1999 that would have reduced inspections, eliminated requirements for hurricane shutters, and removed other safety measures established in Dade County after Hurricane Andrew. However, strong opposition from the insurance industry and the public prevented the codes from being weakened. In 2002 the Florida Building Code was significantly strengthened to require impact-resistant glass or shutters in new buildings. The code also issued new guidelines for roof construction to keep roofs from flying off in hurricane-force winds.

While the evacuations in advance of Andrew worked well, the provision of relief supplies—including food and water—was

A Small Mountain of Debris

Andrew created tons of debris from the human population in former housing and commercial areas: buildings of all kinds, crushed cars and trucks, and trees and shrubs from yards—a total of 70.7 billion cubic feet (2 billion m³) of debris, or enough to build a pyramid six times as big as the Great Pyramid of Giza, Egypt! Andrew had produced a small mountain of trash. Much of it was burned, and the smoke and ash blew over the Everglades, polluting the air breathed by the animals. What was not burned was buried, and the resulting harmful toxins leached into the water table that underlies the Everglades. Water held within the Everglades swampland is part of the water used for drinking by the people of southern Florida. Since the leaching is a slow process, the effects of this buried debris could remain for many years, forcing increased attention to water purification.

disorganized and left many survivors scrambling for basic necessities. In the past, states have typically assumed that the federal government would ride to the rescue after a major natural disaster. However, if the disaster is large like Andrew, local and state governments, which are already on scene, need to be able to step in immediately and provide emergency help.

People are accustomed to having food, power, and water readily available. Most people think that an Andrew-like disaster will never happen to them, so they do not make their own disaster plans. Furthermore, they assume that someone will put everything back together for them quickly afterward. However, no matter how well organized local, state, and federal agencies—as well as organizations like the Red Cross and the Salvation Army—are, they will never be able to meet everyone's needs during a disaster as large as Andrew. Good preparation can ease the way, but it will not fix the resulting loss of roads, utilities, food, and shelter within a few days. Residents of hurricane areas need to be constantly reminded of that fact.

CHAPTER 8

A Decade Later—
A Slow Recovery

Southern Dade County depended for years on low-paying agricultural work. Poverty, substandard housing, and government neglect had plagued the region long before Hurricane Andrew hit. Despite these initial problems, which were compounded by the hurricane, a decade later southern Florida has made an economic comeback, and people are moving back into the area. While some things have changed, however, many of the same circumstances that contributed to the extent of the Andrew disaster remain.

Fishermen's Retreat, a new development of expensive homes on the water in Theriot, Louisiana, has officials and insurers worried that another category 5 hurricane could cause even more damage than Andrew. (Photo courtesy of Associated Press)

What Has Changed?

In the decade since Andrew, a number of changes have enabled Florida to deal more effectively with another hurricane disaster. Stricter and better-enforced building codes, along with a catastrophe fund to back up insurers for losses, mean that Florida will be better able to cope with the aftermath of a major hurricane. However, home insurance is still difficult to find.

Emergency agencies are better prepared to react to a major disaster. The Federal Emergency Management Agency (FEMA) has established regional offices so that it can coordinate relief efforts more quickly. There are also plans in place to rapidly deploy Department of Defense communications equipment, vehicles, and portable kitchens into disaster areas with a minimum of formal requests for assistance. Seeing the need for sharing resources, states in hurricane-prone areas have set up mutual aid agreements, promising to provide immediate assistance to neighboring states when the need arises.

Recognizing the difficulty of providing relief materials in a timely manner, Florida established a relief distribution center near West Palm Beach that can quickly get supplies to the southern part of the state. State employees are now assigned to coordinate with out-of-town utility workers during disasters to speed up the repair of downed power lines and damaged water and sanitation systems. The state also authorized agencies that may be called upon to provide disaster assistance to have open purchase orders ready to use in emergencies. Open purchase orders allow employees to purchase the supplies that they need without waiting for approval that could delay the receipt of the goods.

Rescue workers—who during Andrew found that they routinely lost communications links—have been provided with satellite phones that do not depend on local power grids and with command posts stocked with computers that can keep track of where the rescuers are and what they are doing. Lastly, in 2000

Florida set aside $18 million to improve the safety of shelters and to expand their capacities. State officials are also working with community colleges and universities to identify suitable buildings for use as shelters in emergencies.

One other result of Andrew was the improvement of housing for migrant farm laborers. Earlier housing for migrant farm workers was flimsy and completely unsuitable for human occupation. Andrew blew flat what it did not blow away of this type of housing. Since then, Everglades Village—with 450 new homes, a child-care center, and a medical clinic—has been constructed. Workers now stay year-round, working in the fields during planting and harvesting seasons and working in other occupations, such as construction, during the rest of the year.

What Is the Same?

One critical problem that remains is the lack of a *land-use plan* that would discourage building on the coastline. Residents are still settling in South Florida at a rate of 800 to 900 per day, and they still desire homes that overlook or are very close to the ocean. All these homes are at risk from the most dangerous part of a hurricane: the storm surge.

Despite the money allotted for reinforcing and expanding shelters, South Florida still does not have sufficient numbers of safe shelter spaces. Palm Beach County alone is without emergency shelter for 50,000 people. More work needs to be done so that all evacuees can be sheltered safely.

Finally, the emergency communications network is still not adequate. A major problem encountered after Andrew was that disaster officials were not able to maintain close contact with people working in the field. As a result, sometimes workers were dispatched to places that were not the highest priority. State and local governments can address all these deficiencies, but the effort will take time and a considerable amount of money.

Many Lessons Learned from "the Big One"

Andrew provided many lessons to the residents of Florida and every other state at risk from a hurricane. The primary lesson was that good hurricane preparedness and timely evacuations save lives. Considering the level of property destruction, one would have anticipated a much higher casualty rate. However, death counts were very low, because people heeded the call to leave their homes for shelters. Of course, the low death rates were partly the result of sheer luck: the storm surge could have been larger and could have come farther inland if Andrew had landed in a different spot. The storm surge of a hurricane still causes the most danger to human survival—there is no way to escape it. Preventing

In 2003, South Carolina law enforcement officials performed a drill simulating evacuation procedures to be put into effect in the case of an environmental disaster similar to Hurricane Andrew. (Photo courtesy of Associated Press)

people from building close to the coastline will reduce the amount of property damage and death. Lessons regarding insurance were also learned, as told in the "Ensuring Insurance" sidebar on this page.

Additional building in former swamplands may prevent adequate rescue efforts for people living in these areas. When people live where the water table is high and the elevation is low, floodwaters due to rain or a storm surge can rise rapidly—too rapidly for people to get out. Evacuation plans will need to allow adequate routes out of these areas and more time to complete the evacuations if loss of life is to be avoided.

Rescue and disaster workers also learned that cell phones do not necessarily continue to work after a storm. If the towers that relay the cell phone calls are blown over by the wind or lose power if the electricity fails, then workers will not be able to place calls. Satellite phones, however, always work, because they do not depend on earth-based transmitters that can be knocked down by the storm or stop working when the electricity supply fails.

Lastly, rescue workers, firefighters, and law enforcement personnel learned that it is important to be able to provide directions that do not depend on street signs or landmarks. When signs all blow down, and debris-strewn streets are all that are left, traveling can become very disorienting for emergency personnel who are trying to reach a given location. Using a global positioning system (GPS), which uses signals from satellites to pinpoint locations on a computer screen, allows for quicker response times.

Ensuring Insurance

Another major lesson learned from Andrew concerned the wisdom of spreading the insurance risk to multiple insurers and to the insured residents themselves. If only a few insurers provide homeowner policies for the majority of people hit by a hurricane or other major disaster, then those companies will be at risk of having all their cash assets wiped out. Insurers may need to insist that homeowners have higher deductibles (meaning that a homeowner pays for more of the damage before the insurer pays its part). There may also be caps placed on the amount that insurers will pay to rebuild a home— particularly if it is built in a high-risk coastal zone.

It Could Have Been Much Worse

Even though Andrew caused over $25 billion in damage, the destruction and death toll actually could have been much worse. Chances are that they will be much worse the next time. The paths of most hurricanes cover a much larger area than Andrew did. If a future hurricane follows the same path as Andrew but has a diameter two to three times bigger, it would wipe out Miami, Miami Beach, Key Biscayne, and Fort Lauderdale—areas that have expensive homes and businesses and many people living close together—as well as the towns, agricultural areas, and national parks in southern Dade. Likewise, a hurricane is probably going to make a direct hit on New Orleans sometime—this city is below sea level and will experience catastrophic flooding if the levees are

The foresight of emergency and rescue teams, in addition to the hard work of relief volunteers, kept Hurricane Andrew from being an even worse disaster for the people of Dade County than it actually was. (Photo courtesy of Associated Press)

breached by the storm surge. (The cities most at risk for hurricane damage are discussed in the sidebar "Which Cities Are Most Vulnerable?" below.) Furthermore, because of the increase in population and the values of homes in South Florida, if an Andrew-sized storm were to hit today in exactly the same place, the *insured losses* (not the total losses) would be more than $30 billion—twice the amount insured when Andrew hit. Insurance companies need to be prepared for those kinds of losses.

Which Cities Are Most Vulnerable?

The U.S. cities of Houston, Texas; Miami and Tampa, Florida; New Orleans, Louisiana; and New York City are those most vulnerable to an Andrew-like storm. (Storms like Andrew may *recurve,* or move north along the Atlantic coastline, which puts New York City directly in their path.) If a larger system were to hit one of these areas, property losses would probably reach $50 billion. If a category 5 hurricane were to make a direct hit on Miami, estimates of damage are as high as $100 billion. Eventually, a large hurricane will hit each one of these cities. The resulting damage will make Andrew look like a very small storm, indeed.

CHAPTER 9

Conclusion

Cleanup in the aftermath of Hurricane Andrew took weeks and months to complete, with volunteers making up most of the workforce. In this photograph taken on August 29, 1992, a local church group helps Florida City residents clear debris and build new roofs on their homes. (Photo courtesy of Associated Press)

Andrew could be considered an example of an important hurricane simply because it caused more damage than any other natural disaster that has hit the United States. However, Andrew is important for many more reasons. Andrew—the first hurricane of an extremely slow 1992 hurricane season—was a late season Cape Verde hurricane that was not even expected to "live," much less become one of the most powerful hurricanes to strike the U.S. mainland. A more typical atmospheric pattern would have sent it

curving to the north and east, away from land. Instead, its powerful winds caused significant damage in the Bahamas and Louisiana, and devastating damage in Florida.

Most important of all, Andrew caused relatively few deaths and injuries despite its destructive powers—far fewer than many weaker hurricanes that have struck the United States in the past. Therefore, the preparation for and response to Andrew are just as important to study as the magnitude of the disaster itself. From these came the recognition of the success of mass evacuations of people, the importance of strictly enforcing building codes, and the necessity of emergency relief plans that can be carried out with just a few hours' notice.

Andrew has also been important as a study of nature's response to disaster. The hurricane struck and inflicted heavy damage on five ecologically sensitive areas: three national parks in Florida and the barrier islands and swamplands of Louisiana. Surveying the damage immediately afterward, and at regular intervals thereafter, scientists have been able to piece together the conditions that promote or retard the healing of an ecosystem. With the lessons learned from the effects of this compact, intense, fast-moving hurricane on sensitive terrain, researchers will be ready to anticipate potential damage from future hurricanes and lessen their impact.

As the costliest hurricane on record, Andrew will continue to serve as a benchmark for natural disasters of the future—hurricanes, in particular. Recently upgraded to a category 5 on the Saffir-Simpson scale, Andrew joins Camille in 1969 as a hurricane against which to compare all others. Atmospheric scientists will continue to study it, analyze it with computer simulations, and work to discover its secrets so that they can better predict the track and intensity of future hurricanes before they hit the United States.

Government response in the face of natural disasters will also be compared to that during Andrew. The relief efforts faced many problems in the hours and days after Andrew hit:

The beach at Bill Baggs Cape Florida State Park reopened in 2002. A storm surge from Hurricane Andrew had drowned the beach, making it unsafe for visitors. (Photo courtesy of Associated Press)

miscommunication between government agencies, an inability to rapidly distribute relief supplies, and a lack of coordination among the many different groups trying to provide assistance. The poorest and neediest of the victims were often the least likely to receive help.

The media and the general public were extremely critical of the disaster relief efforts after Andrew. They did not accept what they considered excuses for why clean water, food, medical attention, and shelter were not available to those who needed them. Emergency directors have worked very hard since Andrew to make sure that they will be ready if a major hurricane comes ashore in their area. They know that the plans that they make now, and how they carry those plans out, will mean the difference between life and death, health and disease, and comfort and misery for the people of their states. If those plans work, everyone will have learned the painful lessons of a spectacular hurricane named Andrew.

Time Line

1992

August 16, 2 P.M. (EDT)	A tropical wave in the eastern Atlantic Ocean becomes a tropical depression, with winds of 29 miles (46.6 km) per hour (25 knots)
August 17, 8 A.M. (EDT)	The tropical depression strengthens to become Tropical Storm Andrew, with winds of 40 miles (64.4 km) per hour (35 knots); Andrew heads for the Lesser Antilles
August 17–20	Andrew's forward movement slows, and the storm turns toward the northwest, thus sparing the Lesser Antilles
August 21, 8 P.M. (EDT)	Andrew turns back toward the west; the tropical storm's forward speed increases to 18 miles (29 km) per hour (16 knots); the wind speed increases to 63 miles (101.4 km) per hour (55 knots)
August 22, 8 A.M. (EDT)	After rapidly intensifying for twelve hours, Andrew becomes a category 1 hurricane, with winds of 80 miles (129 km) per hour (70 knots), and heads west
August 22, 11 A.M. (EDT)	A hurricane watch is issued for the Bahamas

Photo courtesy of National Oceanic and Atmospheric Administration/Department of Commerce

Photo courtesy of National Oceanic and Atmospheric Administration/Department of Commerce

August 22, 5 P.M. (EDT)	A hurricane warning is issued for the Bahamas; a hurricane watch is issued for Florida's east coast, from Titusville south through the Florida Keys
August 22, 8 P.M. (EDT)	Andrew becomes a category 2 hurricane, with winds of 103 miles (166 km) per hour (90 knots)
August 23, 8 A.M. (EDT)	A hurricane warning is issued for Florida's east coast, from Vero Beach south through the Florida Keys; Andrew becomes a category 3 hurricane, with winds of 138 miles (222 km) per hour (120 knots)
August 23, 2 P.M. (EDT)	A hurricane warning is issued for Florida's west coast, south of Venice and Lake Okeechobee; Andrew becomes a category 4 hurricane, with winds of 155 miles (249 km) per hour (135 knots); over 1 million people evacuate southern Florida
August 23, 6 P.M. (EDT)	Andrew strikes northern Eleuthera, the Bahamas, with winds of 150 miles (241 km) per hour (130 knots)
August 23, 9 P.M. (EDT)	Andrew strikes the southern Berry Islands, the Bahamas, with winds of 144 miles (232 km) per hour (125 knots)
August 24, 5:05 A.M. (EDT)	Andrew strikes Homestead Air Force Base in Homestead, Florida, with winds of 145 miles (233 km) per hour (125 knots)

Photo courtesy of National Oceanic and Atmospheric Administration/Department of Commerce

August 24, 5 P.M. (EDT)	A hurricane warning is issued for the northern gulf coast, from Pascagoula, Mississippi, to Port Arthur, Texas
August 25, 5 A.M. (EDT)	A hurricane warning is issued for west of Vermilion Bay, Louisiana, to Port Arthur, Texas; over 2 million people are asked to evacuate from southern Mississippi, Louisiana, and Texas
August 25, 11 A.M. (EDT)	A hurricane warning is issued for west of Port Arthur to Bolivar Peninsula, Texas
August 26, 4:30 A.M. (EDT)	Andrew strikes Point Chevreuil, Louisiana, as a category 3 hurricane, with winds of 105 miles (169 km) per hour (105 knots)
August 26, 2 P.M. (EDT)	Andrew is downgraded to a tropical storm
August 27, 2 A.M. (EDT)	Andrew is downgraded to a tropical depression
August 28, 8 A.M. (EDT)	Andrew merges with a frontal system over the mid-Atlantic states and no longer exists as a tropical system

Photo courtesy of Associated Press

Chronology of Hurricanes

The following list is a selection of major hurricanes of the last 150 years.

1864

October 5
Cyclone
India
Over 50,000 killed

1876

October 31
Cyclone
India
200,000 killed

1900

September 8
United States (Texas)
6,000 to 12,000 killed

1906

September 18
Typhoon
China (Hong Kong)
10,000 killed

1926

September 17–18
United States (Florida)
373 killed

1928

September 12–16
Guadeloupe, Puerto Rico, and
    United States (Florida)
3,400 killed

1935

September 2
United States (Florida Keys)
400 killed

1938

September 21
United States (New England
    and New York)
564 killed

Photo courtesy of Associated Press

1942

October 16

Cyclone

India (Bay of Bengal)

40,000 killed

1959

September

Typhoon Vera

Japan

5,000 killed

1963

September 30–October 9

Hurricane Flora

Cuba and Haiti

6,000 killed

1969

August 17

Hurricane Camille

United States (Louisiana and
   Mississippi)

256 killed

1970

November 12

Cyclone

East Pakistan (Bangladesh)

300,000 to 500,000 killed

1979

August 31–September 8

Hurricane David

Dominica, Dominican
   Republic, Puerto Rico, and
   United States (East Coast)

1,457 killed

1985

May 25

Cyclone

Bangladesh

10,000 killed

1988

September 12–19

Hurricane Gilbert

Cayman Islands, British Virgin
   Islands, Dominican
   Republic, Haiti, Jamaica,
   Mexico, Puerto Rico, St.
   Lucia, U.S. Virgin Islands,
   and United States (Texas)

350 killed

1991

April 30

Cyclone

Bangladesh

139,000 killed

November 5

Typhoon Thelma

Philippines

3,400 to 5,000 killed

Photo courtesy of Associated Press

1992

August 22–26

Hurricane Andrew

Bahamas and United States
(Florida and Louisiana)

65 killed

1998

September 20

Hurricane Georges

Cuba, Dominican Republic,
Haiti, Puerto Rico, and
United States (Florida,
Mississippi, and Louisiana)

6,000 killed

October 29

Hurricane Mitch

El Salvador, Guatemala,
Honduras, and Nicaragua

9,000 killed, 9,000 missing

1999

October 29

Cyclone

India

Over 9,500 killed

2003

September 18

Hurricane Isabel

United States (North Carolina
and Virginia)

40 killed

2004

August 9–14

Hurricane Charley

Cuba, Jamaica, and United
States (Florida)

15 killed

August 24–September 9

Hurricane Frances

Bahamas, United States
(Florida)

23 killed

September 2–24

Hurricane Ivan

Grenada, Jamaica, Cayman
Islands, Cuba, United States
(Alabama, Florida,
Louisiana, Mississippi)

90 killed

September 13–20

Hurricane Jeanne

Bahamas, Dominican Republic,
Haiti, United States (Florida)

More than 2,000 killed

Photo courtesy of Associated Press

Glossary

alien plants   Nonnative plants that have been imported from other parts of the world; exotic plants

anemometer   An instrument for measuring wind speed

Atlantic Ocean hurricane season   The period from June 1 through November 30 each year when conditions are right for hurricanes to form in the tropical Atlantic Ocean, the Caribbean Sea, and the Gulf of Mexico

barrier island   An island built entirely of sand that lies offshore and parallel to the coastline

building code   A set of rules for how homes, schools, hospitals, and other buildings must be constructed

convective clouds   Clouds formed by rapidly rising, moist air; thunderstorm clouds found within the hurricane eye wall are convective clouds

ecosystem   A community of plants and animals inhabiting a distinct environment

eye   The clear, calm center of a hurricane

eye wall   The ring of tall, convective clouds that surround the eye; the location of the highest winds in the hurricane

frontal system   The boundary between a warm air mass and a cold air mass that brings rain or snow and wind as it passes over; once a hurricane moves onshore, its energy may be added to that of a frontal system

hurricane   A tropical cyclone with sustained winds of 74 miles (119 km) per hour or greater

hurricane warning   A broadcast advising residents that a hurricane may arrive within 36 hours

hurricane watch   A broadcast advising residents that winds of 74 miles (119 km) per hour will arrive at their location in 24 hours or less

land-use plan   A plan created by local or state governments that describes the kinds of buildings (homes, businesses, factories, schools) that can be built in certain areas

levee   A barrier built on both sides of a river or canal that keeps floodwaters within the channel

marina   A place for docking small boats

reef   A ridge found at or near the surface of the water that may be formed of corals (natural reefs) or human-made objects like wrecked ships or pieces of concrete (artificial reefs); reefs are home to large varieties of marine life

Saffir-Simpson hurricane scale   A scale of 1 to 5 used to place hurricanes into categories based on the hurricane's wind speed and destructive power

storm surge   A high wall of water that comes ashore in advance of a hurricane; it is caused by the hurricane's winds and low atmospheric pressure

subtropics   The areas on Earth that are next-closest to the poles from the tropics

sustained wind   A wind speed measurement that remains constant for one minute

swamp   Wetlands where shrubs and trees are the dominant forms of plant life

tropical cyclone   The general term applied to any low-pressure circulation that originates over a tropical ocean; this term applies to tropical depressions, tropical storms, and hurricanes

tropical depression   An early stage in the life of a tropical cyclone; sustained winds must be between 23 and 38 miles (37 and 61 km) per hour

tropical disturbance   An area of increasing numbers of convective clouds over a tropical region of the ocean; it may develop into a tropical depression

tropical storm   The stage of a tropical cyclone between a tropical depression and a hurricane; sustained winds must be between 39 and 73 miles (63 and 117 km) per hour

tropical wave   An elongated area of low pressure in the tropics

tropics   The area on Earth between the equator and approximately 23.5 degrees of latitude

wetlands   Land saturated with water and home to plants and animals that live in, on, or near water

Further Reading and Web Sites

American Red Cross. This web site discusses preparing for and dealing with the effects of natural disasters. Available online. URL: http://www.redcross.org. Accessed March 22, 2004.

Barnes, Jay. *Florida's Hurricane History.* Chapel Hill, NC: University of North Carolina Press, 1998. A detailed look at over 100 Florida hurricanes, including Andrew.

Bioscience, April 1994. This issue is devoted to the environmental effects of Hurricane Andrew.

Fisher, David. *The Scariest Place on Earth: Eye to Eye with Hurricanes.* New York: Random House, 1994. This book presents scientific information on hurricanes, as well as the author's own experience as a resident of Miami, Florida, during Hurricane Andrew.

FoodSafety.gov. This web site provides links to various federal and state agencies that address issues of food and water safety after natural disasters. Available online. URL: http://www.foodsafety.gov. Accessed March 22, 2004.

Greenberg, Keith. *Hurricanes and Tornadoes.* New York: Twenty-First Century Books, 1994. This book provides basic information on two of nature's fiercest storms—hurricanes and tornadoes.

_____. *Storm Chaser: Into the Eye of a Hurricane.* Woodbridge, CT: Blackbirch Press, 1998. This book tells the story of a U.S. Air Force pilot who flies planes into hurricanes.

Habitat for Humanity International. This web site explains Habitat for Humanity's international homebuilding work. Available online. URL: http://www.habitat.org. Accessed March 22, 2004.

Lovelace, John K. and Benjamin F. McPherson. U.S. Geological Survey (USGS) Water Supply Paper 2425: "Restoration,

Creation, and Recovery—Effects of Hurricane Andrew (1992) on Wetlands in Southern Florida and Louisiana." USGS—National Water Summary on Wetland Resources. This article gives detailed information on how Andrew disrupted habitats in the Everglades and the Atchafalaya River Basin, including those inhabited by reptiles, amphibians, and fish. Available online. URL: http://water.usgs.gov/nwsum/ WSP2425/andrew.html. Accessed March 11, 2004.

Miami Museum of Science—Hurricane: Storm Science. This web site gives scientific information on hurricanes and directions for building a weather station at home. The site also presents the story of a family from Homestead, Florida, that survived Hurricane Andrew. Available online. URL: http://www.miamisci.org/hurricane/index.html. Accessed March 11, 2004.

Moran, Joseph M., and Michael D. Morgan. *Meteorology: The Atmosphere and the Science of Weather.* New York: Macmillan, 1994. This book gives a basic description of the atmosphere, weather, and climate.

Murray, Peter. *Hurricanes.* Plymouth, MN: Child's World, 1996. This book takes the reader through the stages of a hurricane.

National Aeronautics and Space Administration (NASA)— Tropical Twisters—Hurricanes: How They Work and What They Do. This web site provides a scientific discussion of hurricane formation and behavior. Available online. URL: http://kids.earth.nasa.gov/archive/hurricane/damage.html. Accessed March 11, 2004.

National Oceanic and Atmospheric Administration (NOAA)— Hurricane Andrew. Links, photos, images, and interviews about Hurricane Andrew from this government web site. Available online. URL: http://www.noaa.gov/ hurricaneandrew.html. Accessed November 13, 2004.

National Weather Service (NWS)—National Hurricane Center (NHC) Tropical Prediction Center. The NHC web site provides information on hurricane safety, descriptions of past hurricanes, both in the United States and around the world (including satellite photos), and up-to-date information on Atlantic hurricanes during the hurricane season. Available online. URL: http://www.nhc.noaa.gov. Accessed March 11, 2004.

Provenzo, Eugene F., Jr., Asterie Baker Provenzo, and Gary Mormino. *In the Eye of Hurricane Andrew.* Gainesville: University Press of Florida, 2002. This book features interviews with over 100 people who survived Hurricane Andrew.

Salvation Army—International Headquarters. This web site has information on the Salvation Army's relief work around the world. Available online. URL: http://www1.salvationarmy .org/ihq/www_sa.nsf. Accessed March 22, 2004.

Santana, Sofia. "Remembering Andrew." *Weatherwise,* July/August 2003, 14–18. This article, by a *Miami Herald* reporter who lived through Hurricane Andrew, describes the hurricane's arrival and the recovery of South Florida since then.

Schlatter, Thomas. "A Hurricane Primer." *Weatherwise,* October/November 1993, 40–43. This article answers questions about hurricane behavior.

Scotti, R.A. *Sudden Sea: The Great Hurricane of 1938.* Boston: Little, Brown, 2003. This book describes the destructive New England hurricane of 1938.

Sherrow, Victoria. *Hurricane Andrew: Nature's Rage.* New York: Enslow Publishers, 1998. This book discusses Hurricane Andrew's development and path of destruction, and the recovery efforts that followed.

U.S. Army Corps of Engineers—Office of History No. 55 (Hurricane Andrew). This web site describes the efforts made by the South Atlantic Division and the Jacksonville District of the Army Corps of Engineers to provide housing, restore water and electricity, and remove debris after Hurricane Andrew. Available online. URL: http://www.hq.usace.army.mil/ history/vignettes/Vignette_55.htm. Accessed March 11, 2004.

U.S. Department of Homeland Security—Federal Emergency Management Agency (FEMA). This web site discusses natural disasters—including tornadoes, floods, and hurricanes—and how to prepare for them. Available online. URL: http://www.fema.gov. Accessed March 22, 2004.

U.S. Geological Survey (USGS)—LAcoast. This web site provides information on Hurricane Andrew's effect on the barrier islands just off the Louisiana coast. Available online. URL: http://www.lacoast.gov. Accessed March 11, 2004.

U.S. Geological Survey (USGS)—Biological Resources. This web site describes how Andrew affected coastal landscapes—wetlands, barrier islands, and forests. Available online. URL: http://biology.usgs.gov. Accessed March 11, 2004.

WildWeather.com—Hurricane Andrew 10th Anniversary. All of Andrew's statistics are included in a look back at the hurricane on this weather web site. Available online. URL: http://www.wildweather.com/features/Andrewtenth.htm. Accessed November 13, 2004.

Winsberg, Morton. "Measuring Andrew's Aftermath." *American Demographics,* May 1996, 22. This article discusses the migration of people out of Dade County after Hurricane Andrew.

Index

Harris County Public Library
Houston, Texas